Asian Guide

Asian Guide

Leonardo D. Moral

iUniverse, Inc.
New York Lincoln Shanghai

Asian Guide

iUniverse, Inc.

For information address:
iUniverse, Inc.
2021 Pine Lake Road, Suite 100
Lincoln, NE 68512
www.iuniverse.com

ISBN: 0-595-32044-9

Printed in the United States of America

Contents

Preface

I have decided to write this book in order to pass on practical knowledge I have gained growing up in America. I start in the beginning discussing the family unit because of my first hand experience with younger family members. I have observed how their parents do not know the value of teaching their children proper study habits. The parents do not even get involved in their children's homework.

I wish to help future Asian children in their educational goals. The reason is I have seen many young Asians grow up with poor study habits. Many have decided that a good education is not necessary. I hope that they will not concentrate more on having a fun time with their friends in high school and throughout college.

The other major reason I have for writing this book is to help young professionals in their workplace. I myself have encountered many types of people with different attitudes toward Asians. Some of the people feel comfortable with Asians. Other people have very low opinions of Asians. This book will help alleviate some of the frustrations an Asian might feel when they encounter discrimination.

Another reason I have is to educate young professionals to invest in themselves. I want to share my experiences in obtaining patents through my work and not receiving any substantial reward. I want to show the young Asians how to protect their inventions and profit from their innovative products.

Finally, to round off the book, I want to advice Asians on how to present themselves in social settings. This book will serve as a guide for Asians already living in America and those immigrating. The book will help Asians who are not very familiar with American life become well acclimated.

Introduction

I was born in the Philippines in 1959 and attended school there up to the third grade. My parents immigrated to Chicago and brought me here along with my sister when I was ten years old. During that time, I watched many cousins who are second generation Asians grow up in Chicago after their parents had immigrated. I have witnessed how many of them behave poorly in our family gatherings. Even their parents are at times dismayed because of their disrespect for the elders.

I attended the rest of my grammar school and high school in Chicago. During this time, my grandparents and parents have taught me to respect my elders for they do know more than I do. They have taught me to study hard and to finish my college education. They involved me in preparing food and cutting up the various meats and fish. I learned how to cook some of the Filipino food from helping out in the kitchen. I performed house chores ranging from vacuuming to throwing out the trash. Never once did I complain nor shy away from the duties.

I was already taking collegiate courses in my last year of high school. These are college algebra and two psychology courses. During my senior year in high school, I was already researching the colleges I wish to attend. I gathered the information about the test scores I would need. Before attending college, I researched the various ways I could finance the tuition costs.

After graduating college in Mechanical Engineering, I was fortunate enough to work in the suburbs for a telecommunication company. At this stage, I met various people who still harbor discriminatory feelings. I had to learn how to deal with them over the coming years. This is actually when the real acclimation period in the U.S. occurred for me, when I started working. Nevertheless, this did not deter my goal for attending graduate school in my first year at the company. I have received my Master in Mechanical Engineering four years later. I immediately pursued my Master in Business Administration and received it after another four years.

I joined a health club in order to build more strength. The weight lifting rounded my repertoire of sports activities that included tennis and volleyball. It added more strength into the other sports.

During this time, I have occasional breakouts of pimples. I did use commercial lotions and soaps. This did not help me at all. It was then I decided to see a dermatologist to help cure me of breakouts. It was the best thing I have ever done for my facial condition.

I have taken numerous Salsa lessons because of the joy I received in dancing. It helped give me new social skills. I took a Salsa seminar in San Juan in order to learn more Salsa. The trip to San Juan was one of the best vacations I have taken. After many months of dancing, I taught friends and relatives to dance Salsa. I was able to meet many girls in the Latin nightclubs due to my knowledge of Salsa dancing.

Engineers dream of receiving a patent and I am one of them. I have applied and received four patents through work in different companies. Unfortunately, I did not receive any royalties on the money that my patents provide for the companies. This is one of the main reasons I pursued this book in order to share my experiences and to give clear advice.

The good news is that I am using my knowledge of patent application for my own personal product ideas. With luck, I will be able to license the patents. This is a standard personal goal of many creative Asian people, who I can aid with this book.

This book will help you as an Asian whether you are in your teenage years or you are already married with children. This book will act as a simplified guide in helping you in any stage of your life by providing a direct approach in becoming acclimated to the American life. You as a teenager will go through many things in life, such as choosing your friends and career to interacting with your elders. There are many unknown things to you that you will require help from your parents. Moreover, if you should be a parent, this book will help enlighten you with your children's lives and schoolwork.

Some of the chapters deal in helping you as parents to remember to discipline your children properly. Your children should listen to you and follow what you say. There is no excuse for your children not to obey you. Many second generation Asians do not have the slightest idea of how to properly address their elders. They do not even know how to behave with other elders outside of their own family.

Your children may decide not to even pursue a worthwhile career in order to support themselves. They may have no ambition to excel and to provide for themselves after they have left your household. Many children think that because they get all the praises from similar friends that there is no need to get a great profession. Their thinking is very short term and do not care much about the coming future. They lack the proper training in becoming actual responsible adults.

Another chapter will show the misconceptions of parents paying for all the college tuition. This situation calls for a very active involvement from both you and your children in searching for ways to finance the tuition costs. You as a parent may think that you will have to pay for all the tuition costs. This actually causes a lot of stress in your family that it often leads to many arguments. Your children may actually give up on their college education and just start looking for any simple jobs.

Similarly, this book shows you as parents what your children must do in order to find the financial solutions to the tuition costs. Your children must be proactive and do most of the legwork involved in securing money from other sources to finance the tuition. Your children should also be held accountable for the tuition costs because this is tied directly to their grades. Corporations will use their grades as a criterion before hiring them. The hiring manager will obviously hire a person with a better grade point average than someone else.

If you do not educate and discipline your teenagers, they will just rely on you to keep providing for them. They will not have the drive or ambition to further themselves in their careers. Your children will not want to pursue another degree in a graduate study. This is a very sad state because the graduate education is one of the best things your children can receive which will be paid by their employer.

This book talks about an opportunity that must be pursued by your children or yourself. This opportunity is provided to everyone in a company but if your children are not encouraged to study, they will never pursue the graduate degree. They are content in living a fun life with their college friends even during their professional careers.

You may have forgotten your roots. This book also deals in helping you as an individual Asian in behaving properly in your household. You must know what you would need to do in order to help better yourself. This includes on how to behave on dates. Total respect for people must be practiced in order to have a meaningful relationship.

You as an Asian will go through many hard situations in life. A work environment is one of the hardest place in which you will have to endure. There could be many people who may give you hard times because you are an Asian. This book deals with this in a simple manner and shows how to stay out of trouble.

One of the most important topics is how to change stereotypical behaviors that you may exhibit. There are very simple ways to solve these behaviors. This could be as simple as how you dress or wear your hair. Other things are the usual speech mannerism that you can improve.

This book also helps educate you should you be a very creative Asian who may be working for company in a technology field. There are certain ways where you can pursue your own innovative idea and market it under your own name. If you are successful, then your innovative idea could bring in a lot of money from royalties or licensing fees. There is no need for you to keep giving all your great ideas to your workplace. If you did keep submitting your ideas to your workplace, you will never see a dime from it. You will never reap the real reward of collecting money and retiring early.

This book also encourages you as Asians to keep your bodies healthy. There are many ways to do this but this book focuses on a few key items. These include eating habits, physical fitness and even social activities. There is no need for you to have a very elaborate workout schedule in order to remain healthy. Even the simplest act of staying out of the sun is strongly suggested in this book.

Another very important topic discussed is your skin care and treatment for acne and other blemishes. This book clearly shows what you as a parent and person must do to help your children and yourself in case of acne. There really is no need to waste time by using common lotions and other things that may be found in the pharmacy. By following the suggestions, your skin condition can be treated permanently without wasting too much money and time.

Overall, this book deals with various topics in a straightforward manner and does not elaborate into every detail. Hopefully, you and your family in reading this book will benefit greatly in all your current stage of life. This book will also help you see that there are certain things you can do to your children in order for them to be more successful in their lives.

1

Family Values

Parents with Young Children

In today's society, many things can go wrong in a family unit. Parents want the best for their children. This includes education, their future wife and raising their own family. They want the children to be successful and have a good career in order to support themselves. They would not want their children to become criminals and spend time in jail. Raising good successful children starts with the family.

A strong Asian family unit is very important. One day you and your spouse may eventually become parents. As parents, you must hold everybody together and provide a place where your spouse and children can feel safe. Your family as a whole must be always be together and support each other. There must be constant respect between you, your spouse and your children.

You must be strong and teach your children well about the Asian family background and customs. They must learn the good family values that you have already learned. There is nobody else that can do this for your children other than you. This is a never-ending obligation in teaching your children.

You must discipline your children and teach them the proper way to address their elders. The children must know that you and your spouse are working very hard to provide them the necessary food and shelter. They must realize that money does not come very easily and that it requires you two to work extremely hard. You must let your children know whatever sacrifices you have made in order for them to have a roof over their heads.

You and your spouse can stop your children from becoming disrespectful. You can put them on the proper path again, as when they just started first grade. You and your spouse must be good role models for your children. You can do this by always showing your children the right things to do. Speak clearly with them and do not use curse words. Treat them with high respect and show them how good that makes them feel.

You must be kind to your children and help build up their self-esteem. Praise them for their work and good behavior around your household whenever you have a chance. Just imagine when you were a child and how you have felt when your parents praised you. This is something that you can pass onto your children. One of the main things you can do is to let your children win in some games that you play with them. There is no need for you to keep winning because you are an adult. Your children will benefit more by knowing they can accomplish something in a good-natured manner. They will develop confidence in themselves and have a better outlook in life.

Early childhood study habits are one of the most important behaviors your children must learn early in time. This is when they should be getting into a routine of sitting down by a study table with proper lighting. They must learn to focus their attention in their studies no matter how easy it is. This will train your children to keep their minds on the task they need to accomplish. One great thing you can do is to encourage your children to study as soon as they get home.

You must give your children incentives on getting good grades. Reward them with praises, trips to the movies, fun toys, or a nice dinner in their favorite restaurant. You can even use money as a reward when they are at the correct age. Your rewards will help reinforce the behaviors of achieving good grades. It will reinforce all the valuable things they will need in their development towards adulthood.

You must have your children help you around the house by doing some chores. Make sure your children work with their hands in helping to prepare food and cleaning up the dinner table. Have your children do the house cleaning and yard work when they are old enough. Let them clean the bathroom and throw out the garbage.

Show your children the skills that they would need around the kitchen also. You must teach them how to clean and prepare a chicken, meat and even fish. No matter how much they may complain, make sure that your children help you out in the food preparation.

When you do make your children help around the house, do it in a calm and nice manner. Do not approach it in an angry mood. Showing anger will just make them feel uncomfortable. They will just resist and procrastinate. All you really have to do is persuade them in a calm manner.

Communicating with Your Children

The key is constant communication with your children. There are many ways you can make the children listen. There are the traditional restrictions to watching television or hanging out with friends. Monitor their educational progress by checking every report card. This is your duty and right as a parent. Question your children if the grades are very low. Observe their study habits and make sure they are following it. Do not be discouraged. At times, they will not listen, but if you speak to them in a serious manner, they will start to listen.

You must become involved with your children's academic activities. Check their homework and ask about what they are learning. Do not just sit back and let the children do their homework alone. Pick some topics and ask your children's opinion. Have a small discussion or debate about something from their homework.

You must tell your children to respect their elders. Teach them to answer questions properly. They must learn good manners. Let them know the family's history and how their grandparents have lived their lives. Expose them to all the cultural activities you can remember or go to local city events. Involve them in your travels back to your homeland. Take them and show them all the old neighborhoods where everyone used to visit. Let them see for themselves the beauty of their home country and their roots. Let them stay for weeks with their relatives and they will fully appreciate it. They may even start to learn speaking their actual native language. This usually happens with some children who go back to their homeland. The children are immersed in the country and all the people they will have to interact.

If you did not follow your cultural customs, you will not know it and you will not pass it down to your children. They could even have more rebellious children than themselves and not know how to deal with them. Their own family unit will eventually break apart which will lead to the usual divorce as a final solution.

They will struggle in their own family unit and they will be consumed by the problems. They definitely will have problems especially if they have been a braggart during their teenage years. They think they know everything but in actuality lack the essential skills to keep a family together.

When you do try to tell your children to behave properly, they will rebel and give you all sorts of excuses. Be ready to hear these excuses and try very hard to discern which ones are believable. The main thing you must remember is to listen objectively and choose the right decisions to help your children grow up properly.

However, the sad thing is that many parents do not know what to do. Some parents are not strong enough to deal with this situation. Alternatively, it could be they are relying on other people to fix their problems for them. You must remember as a parent that you must do something. Do not be shy to talk to your children.

When you see these behaviors and lack of respect from your children, you must stand up to them and correct them. As a responsible parent, you must stop the behaviors. You can talk to your children and tell them that you will not accept any disrespectful behaviors. You have all the rights as a parent to teach your children how to behave in the home and society. You should not be afraid of your children.

You can seek help from other relatives or local governmental agency. If you do nothing, then your family unit will actually be weakened and ultimately break-down. Do not put on a front with your other relatives trying to show off your children as being smart and successful when in fact they are not. There is no honor in standing behind your children if they are just trying to get by life on free ride from you. This gives your children the false impression that they are smart enough to be on their own. They will actually prefer to gain the respect from their friends by showing them how they can stand up against you and your spouse. This includes total disrespect to you and your spouse.

When you start experiencing any hint of disrespect from your children, you must act as a parent and discipline your children. You must tell your children what they are doing wrong in a stern voice. It is acceptable for you to get involved and to be angry at this stage because it is your parental right. Do not be afraid to be angry with your children when they start exhibiting bad behaviors.

For example, I myself got involved when I noticed one cousin, who was in high school, mouthing off about his parents and totally disrespecting them. He was acting very conceited and being a braggart. He was actually calling his parents bad names. All this was going on during a family holiday gathering. At some point, I told him off using exactly his kind of language in a very stern and angry voice. At that time, I did not care who was around or who heard me. Later, his mother came to me and thanked me for straightening him.

Parents' Behavior

As a parent, you must still be respectful of your own parents and elders both in your immediate family and outside the family. Do not be a braggart as a person or even about your own children. There is no need to tell everybody how great your children are doing in school. You could just be setting yourself for a big disappointment. The final reward is when your children actually graduate from college and gets a respectable job. You will have the peace of mind that your children will be able to support themselves.

You must stay on course in your life's journey. Be true to yourself and your immediate family. Do not take advantage of anybody both family and close friends. The good family habits discussed should become second nature. You should give respect without even thinking about it. The good things that you give to other people will eventually come back to you.

You must lend a hand to anyone who needs help even if he/she do not ask. When they ask you to do some simple tasks, do the tasks well. Do not give a half-hearted attempt since it will show in your work. You must always help the underprivileged people.

Show respect to your family first and always put them ahead of friends. Your family will be the only people that will be there in your darkest hours. People may have fun with friends but when they become gravely stricken, they will not always be there. They will not help the person go to the toilet should he become handicapped. Only the family members will be doing these kinds of labor. This is why nobody should put their friends in front of their family.

Dealing with Bad Relatives

Although you and your spouse may have great family values, you will have inconsiderate relatives. These types of relative will take advantage of your family and consequently influence your children. These bad relatives will always think they are doing the correct actions. They think that the world revolves around them. Study these kinds of relatives. Observe how they speak and act. You will be able to tell the difference of which relatives will be true to you and in their hearts. There are many signs and clues that will help you read your family.

One sign to observe how the parents act in these bad family units. Many children will often exhibit their parent's habits whether they are good or bad. Notice how both parents and child treat each other and strangers. Listen to how they talk about people. Observe how they possibly speak badly of strangers or spread unfounded rumors. Watch how someone known to be truly good reacts to bad rumors. Compare how good people behave in social situations against crude relatives. This will further help teach which relatives have completely bad traits and take advantage of their family members.

The reason for the lesson in finding out which relatives are bad is to help you in how to deal with them. Never put yourself in a situation where people can take advantage of you and your children. Do not volunteer too many actions or help to them. They will take the opportunity and actually take more than what you offered. Be careful also and do not believe everything that they say or do

Remember these kinds of relatives do not care about other people. They are the braggart and selfish types of family members. They will berate and ridicule people and immediate family members. They are quick to call people names and their insults will eventually filter onward. This is how they live, by making fun of people instead of helping them.

Now that they are exposed, you can disregard them and their comments. Just say brief salutations to them at family gatherings and walk away from them. Let them fight among their own kinds. Go seek out the truly good relatives or one's own immediate family members. You will spend better time with them and find it more rewarding.

At times, some people will want to take up their roots and get away from distant relatives but cannot do so. They would not really have to do that if they remember to be strong and that they have their own mind. Some may eventually find out that they do not need the bad relatives in their lives. They will find that their own immediate family members will be there to help. In this manner, the bad relatives can never take advantage of other family members.

Growing Up in Your Parent's House

If you are still living with your parents, you must perform the household chores. Even if your parents do not ask, you should do this. You must do this in a regular manner. Help cook in the kitchen whenever food is being prepared. Take out the garbage and clean all the bathrooms. Go and do the grocery shopping with your mother.

Your own parents should have passed the good family values to you. Your parents should have shown you and the rest of your siblings how to respect your elders inside the family. This is such an important lesson that it cannot be stressed enough. Someone must have taught you to respect the elders outside the immediate family. These could have been your aunts, uncles and friends of the family.

You should know how to prepare and cook your own native foods. You can buy just about all the ingredients in Asian stores in the U.S. You can learn that much more about your cultural background and begin to appreciate its richness.

Someone will ask you about the foods in your native region and if you actually know how to make them.

Knowing how to cook will come in very handy when you start entertaining your family and friends. There will be times when you might want to hold a family holiday dinner and even birthday parties. Here, everyone usually brings a dish so that you do not have to cook the entire meal. You will have any problems because you will know how to make a dish.

You also learn how to shop for the freshest meat and produce in the market place. You will not feel helpless and be intimidated about buying spices. At some point, you will even use your cooking experience in preparing other types of dishes. You could easily make lasagna; stir fry some meat and vegetables; or even just barbecue some ribs. The skill you develop will keep you from eating a lot of fast food. It will help you stay healthy.

If you are not married yet, there will come a time when you will have to cook for a date. This could be as simple as roasting a chicken or making omelets. Your date will be impressed on how well you can move around the kitchen and prepare something wonderful. People will appreciate your efforts and work.

In addition, when you have friends visit, you will never experience stress in the kitchen. You will know what to serve the people. You will truly become a good host who can provide something nice for your friends. They will have great respect for you as you can provide good things to eat.

As an Asian, you cannot lose yourself and become astray in your life. Your parents must pass on down the family values that make Asians distinct. These values are what attract other ethnic background to Asians. They know that Asians can be trusted and will maintain a good household. All this is true especially for first generation Asians. For second generation Asians, it will take a little more luck to find such a household.

Problems with Teenagers

The problem these days is that many second-generation Asian teenagers growing up in America have no real respect for their elders. They have lost themselves in their circle of friends and have no regard anymore of their cultural background. Their friends could be from their native country but they do not really fully acknowledge it. They will ridicule some of the family customs, the food that they eat, slight tinge of cultural accent and even at times will start making fun of how people look. You can easily identify these behaviors.

For example, one of my cousins has totally taken advantage of his mother by taking as much money as he can. He has made many excuses such as not being able to pay his car payments because he has to support his wife and kids. Similarly, this cousin is one of those teenagers that keep bragging about how much money he is making from his job.

The sad thing is not too many people seem to take the disrespectful behavior seriously enough. These teenagers are the ones that totally have no respect for their parents, friends and themselves. They like to make fun of other people because they want to feel bigger than anyone else does. They feel a need to be always better than anybody else does, but without doing any real work or major accomplishments. These teenagers typically exhibit bragging behaviors, even if they are already failing their college exams.

These teenagers are the ones who do not like to study. They are always trying to push the successful students down beneath them. They think that by doing this they are above everyone else. These teenagers have lost their self-esteem. They will eventually become rebellious. You could see this in other Asian families that are failing. The children are always disobeying their parents and will often fight back. What will happen is that they may find work somewhere but they will go on badmouthing their supervisors.

One example is another cousin who never finished his college degree but has a tremendous disregard for the elders in his family. He also has no respect for himself and other people who have more authority over him. He would even go as far to ridicule his own friend who is now his boss.

These lost teenagers are rejecting their cultural background. They feel ashamed of their customs. They do not like how their parents present themselves. They think that be rejecting and making fun of their own family members, they are that much closer to their non-Asian friends.

They are too materialistic and just want to have a good time with their peers. They like to attend many parties and try to look good to everyone. They do not have any care in the world. They will not care what other people may think of their behaviors. Many of the teenagers tend to brag a lot and care more for their friends than their immediate family members. This is very prevalent in many families.

They also put on good appearances that they do like their cultural background. They do this by hanging around friends from their country or by joining a school club for Asians. They go through the motions of bringing some food at the functions. This is the extent of it. In reality, they just go to the functions for the house dance parties that follow. It is another way for them to party some more without being lectured.

How to Treat Your Spouse

As for the spouse, make sure that they get the proper respect. There is nothing more damaging than the both parents fighting. Letting your children see the fight will only contribute to your children's disrespecting behavior. You and your spouse must be good to each other and not stray. You and your spouse have taken vows to honor each other, which you must do. Follow these simple guidelines and your family unit will be successful.

You must never cheat on your spouse with another person. You must never perform "emotional infidelity" with another person. The meaning is for you not to go out and enjoy another person's company while your spouse is sitting alone at home or at work. This is just as damaging as an actual physical infidelity. There is no excuse where you enjoy somebody else's company than your spouse'. You may come up with many reasons but these are just excuses, which you are using to justify your "emotional infidelity". Your spouse is probably sitting at home crying on the inside.

Eventually, you will perform physical infidelity by sleeping with this person. By then you would have justified your actions further by saying that you have something more in common with the other person.

Treat your spouse to a nice surprise occasionally. This goes both ways. Take each other to a nice restaurant that you each have discovered. Go dress up and soak up the whole city's ambiance. You will be surprised to find new great places where you can go to eat and have fun with each other. Other ideas could be taking up ballroom dancing lessons. Many places teach dance lessons. This will enrich both your lives as you go on learning. It is also beneficial to your health. Dancing is a form of calisthenics in the most enjoyable type. Time will go unnoticed as you both enjoy yourselves.

In social events, never argue with your spouse no matter if you are correct. There is no point in it if both of you are becoming stressed out in public and starting to disrespect each other. Remember you must yield sometimes to your spouse. You are honoring their feeling, which is very important.

Always be with your spouse if you are having dinner with friends. Never leave your spouse alone. Do not look at other men or women when you are both enjoying yourselves. This type of behavior is very hurtful and can lead to many family arguments. Keep your undivided attention to your spouse. It does not mean ignore everybody else, but just show everyone that you and your spouse enjoy being with each other. Show them the truth of how much respect and love you two have for each other.

Do not be obnoxious or talk loudly. There is no need for you and your spouse to drink heavily in a social gathering. You do not have to show off your accomplishments and success. People do perceive all these to be bad behaviors and will actually connect it to all Asians. Do not give them reasons to think that Asians are irresponsible in public. Do not disgrace yourself, your spouse and your country.

2

Children in School

Grammar School

You must always be involved with your children's activities when they are attending grammar school and even high school. They will not know many things in the world. They will not know how to act properly with other people in a social setting. They will not know which people are trustworthy and which ones will do them harm. Some of these people may even be your very own relatives. They may not do them physical harm but there are some that may take advantage of your children. For example, they could borrow things and money and never return them.

You must show your children the proper way to address their elders with respect. However, you must also show which elders that are actually are being kind to you and your children. Remember there may be some relatives that will not have your best interests in mind. These types of relatives have lost themselves and their honor.

You must show your children the trustworthy people and the dishonest people. You must educate your children to learn about the basic principles of good and evil. They will need your help in learning about the right and wrong things in life. It is up to you to educate them in choosing the right path always and to stay away from doing bad things. You must help them get strong in resisting bad temptations. These could be the usual bad habits that every parents dread which are: taking drugs; stealing money and other things; smoking cigarettes and marijuana; drinking alcohol; driving recklessly; cursing repeatedly to anyone; getting involved sexually while still in high school; joining street gangs; putting their friends in front of their own family; and prostituting themselves. You must teach your children that they must do the right things in life. This will help them stay out of trouble wherever they go and throughout their adult life.

If you do not show them the consequences of making a bad decision, they will keep on getting into trouble. If you are lucky, you may be able to save them from getting into bad situations that can get worse. However, you will not be there all the time. That is why it is imperative that you have an open relationship with your children.

You must teach your children to stay away from strangers at all times. You can see many cases on television where children have been abducted. You would not want this to happen to you when you were a child. You definitely would not want it to happen to your children. You must take all the necessary steps to make sure your children never get into that situation. Whenever you can, you must always take your children to school and pick them up when the classes are over. You must talk to the teachers and watch how they act around the children. Make sure you are comfortable enough with the teachers and that you can trust them.

You must do the same scrutiny for your baby sitters, religious teachers, and even friends of the family. There are so many people that your children will interact and they must all be checked. You need to make sure you can trust them. For the same reason, you must show that you are watching how they treat your children.

Nothing in this world is perfect, so always make sure that people treat your children properly in school. You must always talk to your children to make sure they are not being mistreated or abused at school. No matter what type of school your children are attending, you must make sure they are safe in that environment. Always ask your children how they liked their class everyday. Do not think that this is too ridiculous of a job for you. You will find this to be one of the most important things you can do to ensure your children's safety.

You must always keep your eyes on your children whenever you are out shopping in a mall. You must also have current pictures of your children at all times in case of emergencies. You must also look out for them and know where they are at all times during your family vacations. Make sure you remember what they are wearing whenever you go out. It only makes sense to dress them in bright colors so that you can easily see them in a crowded place.

The bright clothes are also necessary so that drivers can easily see your children. Any bright color will work just as long they are noticeable. You must teach your children not to run into the streets especially between parked cars. This often happens whenever they are playing with a ball and it rolls into the street. They will instinctively go after a ball all the time and dart into the street between parked cars without looking. The drivers will not have enough time to stop and can seriously harm your children.

You must tell your children that they must finish their homework. However, they should do so while putting a great effort in understanding the lessons. You must get involved with them when they are doing their homework. In fact, do the homework with them so that they will have a better comprehension.

You can help by explaining the answers to them. You can describe and give further examples of the answers. Do not think of this as wasting your time. Do not think that it is better for your children to learn by themselves. Your children will not learn the material. Your involvement in your children's education is very critical because they do and will listen to you.

You must show your children by example how they should do their homework. Sit down with them whenever it is time for them to do their schoolwork, no matter what it is. By doing this, you are also going through the motions of good study habits. This is so necessary to learn when they are at the young stage in their development. This good study habit will help them get through high school and college. Your children will excel in their work and get the necessary good grades to succeed.

You must provide your children a good study environment. Get them a nice study table and a comfortable chair. Make sure your children have adequate lighting to read their textbooks without straining their eyes. You must buy a desk lamp if this will help provide the necessary light. You must place it in the house where nothing will distract your children by T.V. and other family members.

Make sure that your children do not over indulge in watching television and playing video games. Monitor how much time they spend talking on the telephone with their friends. Make sure they are not playing all the time or going out to the malls with friends. You must tell them to do all their homework first as soon as they get home from school. In fact, tell your children to come home at a certain time so that they stay out too late. They must endure these small sacrifices.

You must never be angry with your children if there are some mistakes in their homework. What you must do is to sit down with your children and determine where they need improvement. You may discover that one of your children may need more practice in doing the multiplication table. This will be easy for you to resolve. Make your child start with basic by writing it all out as practice. You can then quiz your child later after studying for about an hour. By quizzing your child, you are helping reinforce what he has learned.

The real key to getting good grades is just plain memorization. You must teach your children to memorize the multiplication table perfectly forwards and backwards. Your children may complain but it is for their own good. Explain to them how good it really works and that it will take some time. Your children will do it as long as you are present and involved with the process.

The memorization method is also true for all the subject matters in their school. You must help your children memorize some key topics in the assigned chapters. This will take some effort also but is worthwhile in the end. One way to do this is to have your children read the text maybe two to three times until they remember the key contents. Once they have memorized just about all the information, your children will be able to answer the test questions without too much problems.

This method is also very useful in high school and especially in college. This will help them tremendously to pass all the exams instead of failing or dropping any classes. Your constant tutoring will pay off because your children will not experience stress. Your children will soon realize that you have been telling them the truth about using good study habits.

You must always be involved with your children's social life. You must know who their friends are and what their views are about their own future. You must educate your children to stay away from unscrupulous friends and to focus on their studies. Never give up on this. You must always check their grades because you do not want them to start failing. The funny thing with children is that if they can get away from doing a lot of work, they will do so.

You must be a good role model for your children. They will listen to you and will imitate you often. You must show them that you value education highly and that you yourself have gone through a lot of hard work to get your education. You must always tell your children that having a good education is very necessary in order to make a good honest living. You must tell them that they must study hard in order to be successful in school.

You must tell your children that they must attend a university in order to get a great college education. You must also tell them that they must get their graduate degree while working for a company. Your children must do this especially when the company will pay for the tuition costs. They must do this immediately after graduation while they retain their good study habits.

High School

When your children are in high school, you must tell them the same things about the doing their homework first. You must also tell them that they cannot go out partying when they have schoolwork to finish. You must tell them to stay at home on Friday and Saturday nights studying instead of going out with their friends all the time. Your children must have the discipline to stay home and study.

You must learn to say no to your children when they ask for permission to stay out late at night. This is where you must be strong more than ever. You will be in situations where your children will start to challenge your wishes. The children will crave treatment as adults and more freedom. Do not fall into the misconception that your teenage children can be totally trusted. This is not the case. They can still get into trouble by having bad things come to them.

Never ever, allow them to go out during the weeknights. This is not appropriate when they have responsibilities to finish high school. Never ever, allow them to go out of state for a road trip and to party anywhere. You may think that they are old enough and that you want them to make up their own minds but this usually does not work. This will only cause you a lot of grief and trouble.

Many of the teenagers just want to have fun without thinking about their future. They think they have the right to make their own decisions. Unfortunately, they lose themselves when they start listening more to their friends who are allowed to party too much. Your children will start to pick up these bad habits from friends who do party a lot and who are allowed to go on road trips.

Tell your children that many bad things can happen when they are away from home. They may get into a car accident or become the target of a thief. Your children's money can be stolen from their hotel rooms. Moreover, by being away from your adult supervision, they will become braver and start to do more things without thinking of the consequences. The worst consequence is that your children can end up losing their lives.

They may start to experiment with drugs during a spring break party. They can also start drinking very heavily because of peer pressure. The peer pressure is a very powerful force for any teenagers that have not fully mastered themselves. Your children's friends will band together and call them names if they do not go with them out of state for the spring break.

In order to better prepare your children from bad peer pressures, they must be very comfortable with their decision knowing that it is the right thing to do. Your children must know that they have their own minds and they should know more than their friends should what is good for them. Your children must stand by their correct decisions. Your children must have good self-esteem at all stages of their development. You can help tremendously by giving them compliments when it is due. You need to show pride in their accomplishments no matter how trivial it may seem. Talk to them whenever you do see something they have done. Again, these could be good grades from school or even some house chores they have decided to tackle. Because of your sincere support and honest praises, your children will believe in themselves. They will learn the values that you are teaching them.

They must learn not to listen to their friends who are trying to tempt them into doing something uncomfortable. They must know that in order to be viewed as a mature adult, they must do the right decisions that you have been teaching them. When your children become smarter and really start to understand the values of good judgment, they can withstand the constant peer pressure of doing something irresponsible. For example, your children will not feel obligated to follow their peers to smoke cigarettes or marijuana.

You must instill in your children that they need to learn first how to make good decisions in order to gain more freedom. Tell them that when they can accomplish these things, then they can be trusted more. The main reason you do not trust your teenagers is that they will make irrational decisions even if you have taught them otherwise. You must tell your children that if they can exhibit good behaviors and make mature decisions, then you can trust them more at a comfortable level.

By always communicating and teaching your children to do the right things, you can even help dissolve the so-called rebellion period. This will make your life easier. You will find that your children will not go through this phase just to get some control over their lives. You will not have to fight all the time with them about being not old enough to make their own decisions. You children will understand what they have to do and how to behave in your household.

You will be giving your wisdom to your children by being at their side and making them listen to you. They will understand the ways of the world through your teachings and obviously, from what they see and feel from their environment. This includes all the T.V. shows, movies, news, and other people they meet. You must be at their side all the time when they start becoming exposed to all these things.

3

College

Parents

Many Asian teenagers seem to be at a loss in fulfilling their educational goals and obligations. This is more prevalent when it comes to getting their college degree. They are lost and do not understand that a college degree is essential for a good professional career. At times, they feel that going to college is not important because they have their parents to keep providing for them.

Many parents are not involved and are just not interested in their child's college education. They think that their children know what to do for the college education. They will sit back and let time go by until the very last minute. These parents will often let their children apply to a community college in hopes not paying high tuition costs. Some just simply do not want to pay the tuition and instead persuade their children into applying to very cheap colleges and universities. The parents have the misconception that they have to pay for their entire child's college tuition.

The parents who do not get involved in their children's education will never know the many possible ways for their children to be accepted into an accredited university. This includes the various ways tuition costs can be financed. The parents must read up on the university's pamphlets and other provided brochures.

Therefore, this chapter is directed specifically to your teenager children. After you have read this, you must let your children read this also. The information contained here is very important and must be clearly understood by your children. This section shows all the steps your teenager must do in order to help pay for the college tuition.

Teenagers Going to College

You must get your college degree in order to earn a good salary and support yourself. There is nobody that will give you money to survive. Your friends will not give you a weekly salary to pay for your bills. No matter how much you bond with your friends, giving you money free is the last thing on their minds. They will say many supporting things, but remember actions speak louder than words.

Your parents cannot assume any of your debts as you go through life. When you are with your friends, you undoubtedly talk about wanting more freedom. You and your friends want adult treatment. You feel that you have many good ideas and can make decisions on your own. You feel that you are intelligent enough to get through life and earn a good living.

Then prove it. You must be an adult and assume responsibility for your life. Attend a university and get your bachelor degree in something substantial. Get your degree in engineering, law, medicine, business, or computer science. Show your parents that you can accomplish this goal. No matter what your friends or other people say, finish your degree within four years. Do not take a break or become distracted with trivial things. Do not use the excuse of taking time off and finding yourself. This is meaningless.

College Acceptance Tests and Applications

Getting a college education in the United States is very easy and affordable. You must apply up to five universities that you would really want to attend. This is where getting good grades in high school counts. Universities will look at these grades in order to assess your application. Depending on which university you want to attend, you will need to take some national standardized tests and acquire certain grades. Two of these tests are the American College Test (ACT); the College Board Scholastic Aptitude Test (SAT). Make sure that you study for these tests. Do not waste the opportunity to get the necessary high scores. Otherwise, you would have wasted time and money.

You must do a lot of reading and research in the universities you want to attend. There are numerous literature and brochures regarding student aid and possible scholarships. You must do so much research but it will be worth the time and effort. If the universities you want to attend are close to your home, then you must make every effort to go to the admissions office. Bring a list of questions for the people working there. They will be more than happy to help you get the scholarships.

Call ahead and make an appointment with a guidance councilor for a more personal help. The councilor will give you the appropriate scholarships that may fit your profile. They will instruct you further on how to fill out the forms and where to send them. They will become valuable contacts for you in the future, as you go through the application process. They will give you advice on the types of test and test scores you would need to qualify for the university.

You can use your high school as a resource also. The high schools will have college listings and the corresponding admittance requirement. The high school faculty will also help guide you in the proper direction. They may even know someone at the university with whom they can introduce to you.

Financial Aid and Scholarships

Go to the public library for additional research data. There are materials readily available about companies that offer special grants and scholarships. You must pore over anything that interests you. Always sign up for anything that looks promising.

You can go into the internet and search for possible scholarships. Apply to each and every offer that you think apply to Asians, minorities, special vocation (if you have one), and undergraduate study. Just like in the library, search also various large corporations and small private companies that have scholarship programs. Applying will not cost you anything. It just takes a little of your time.

Some may require you to interview with them. You must go to these interviews prepared and well groomed. If you are male, make sure you are wearing a suit and tie. If you are female, wear appropriate business attire such as blouse, blazer and long skirt. In either case, be a professional in the interview and be articulate. You must behave as a responsible adult. You are not applying to attend a grade school.

Take down all the names, phone numbers, and addresses of the contacts of your applications. Make a working list for the status of your application and possible follow up calls. Make an effort to write thank you letters after the interviews and upon the scholarship approval

Even when you have received more than enough money for your first choice university, keep applying for the scholarships. You may decide to attend a higher priced university. At least you will be more than prepared. In addition, university tuitions keep increasing every year. The extra scholarship money will be able to cover the tuition increase.

You must always fill out the forms for both student aid and scholarship every semester. The student aid can be state funded or come from a bank. Receiving a student loan from a bank is still a good way to pay for the tuition. Depending on the bank and current procedures, the interest rate charge is low and the payments will not start until the student has graduated. You should include the cost of books and other school related items when filling out the student loans.

Collecting the scholarship and loan forms is your responsibility. You must start the process repeatedly every year. Save copies of the last forms in order to help you fill the forms for the next year. Your parents will just have to fill in some minor information. The rest is up to you. Always prepare these forms ahead of time. Do not be late in filling the forms and mailing them. Otherwise, you will not get the money.

Most parents do not know the information above. It is possible for the tuition costs to be covered by scholarships and student loans. You must be responsible enough to seek out all the potential contributing institutions. You must fill out all the forms. You must plan to pay off the loans on your own after your graduation.

Summer Jobs

You must get summer jobs every year to earn extra money. Get the jobs in the direction of your college major. Getting experience towards your career will help you be hired faster upon graduation. Take each job very seriously and professionally. Learn as much as you can. Doing all these things frees your parents from paying any tuition costs.

Universities have placement programs where you can see the type of position available in a company. You must take this if it is available. Try to work for different types of companies every year to broaden your skills. The summer jobs that you do will look great in your resume. Keep the names and phone numbers of your supervisors and colleagues. You will need these as references for your professional job.

Some universities also offer co-operative programs. You alternate working for a company and doing your semester study. This is also appealing and would be very good for you to take because the company will hire you on a permanent basis. Do not be afraid of this program. It may lengthen your year in college maybe by one year but at least it ensures you a job after graduation. Otherwise, go the normal route of getting summer jobs.

Good Study Habits

You must have a good study habit when you start attending college. You must have a good study desk in an area where you will not be distracted. You must take the maximum allowable hour workload in order to finish within four years. Stay focused on your homework and in finishing it in a timely manner. Never put off your homework to watch movies or talk to friends. Do not go out dancing, drinking or partying, especially on a Friday and Saturday night. You must use all the available study time for learning your courses. Even if you think you have done enough, go back and recheck your work. Sometimes you will find some errors or you may just improve the answer, depending on the subject.

You will be getting your first college exam within two to three weeks after the start of the semester. The university usually rotates the exams every week. You must be prepared for the first wave of exams. You do not want to be caught off guard. Once the exams start, more will follow. There will be another exam for a different subject the following week. Meanwhile, you still have homework to do in the other courses. You may even have lab work to do which will take up more of your time.

When you have finally gone through the first wave of exams, two to three weeks will pass until the next wave of exams start. This will continue all the way to the finals. All the grades in the exams and homework add up to your final grade. Take these grades very seriously. They affect your grade point average which all hiring companies use as a hiring tool. There is no way out of this. This is why you must study hard and should not become distracted.

No matter how many times your friends beg or taunt you, do not go out for a joy ride into the city. This is especially true if they are going out of state for fun. Nothing good will ever come from a road trip during your college school days. Your mental discipline will go away and you will become just like your friends who cannot finish college. Never go with your friends for a spring break road trip.

By seeing, some friends who do not finish college may lead you to believe this is acceptable. This is very wrong. You must finish your studies and get your college degree. Never allow yourself to go down to their level of not having an education. You are the only person in the world who can make yourself successful and get that college education. You have to be very serious about it. Do not be aloof, as some misguided Asians have become. You will not succeed in your career path.

You must never ever cheat on your exams. There is no good reason for cheating. All it really takes is to study hard and understand the subject matter. Yes, it is possible. Thousands of other disciplined Asian teenagers are graduating across the nation. There are even more graduating in Asian countries such as the Philippines, Vietnam, China, and Japan. These people are doing this without any excuses. The tuition in some of the universities in these countries is even harder to pay. Think about it. All the people there want to immigrate into the U.S. in order to have a better education and job opportunity. They want to work here to achieve more in their lives.

It is typically better not to have a relationship during your college years. It is all right to date once in awhile but not everyday or every week. Your attention will be taken away from studying. If something should go wrong, you could become broken hearted. This will affect your study habits and grades dramatically. There will be plenty of time for socializing, dancing and dating after college.

Collegiate Responsibilities

Remember you must pay for your own tuition through the scholarships and student loans. If you do not get the good grades, it will be very hard for you to recover the money. You will never recover the time lost. In fact, you will lose even more time because you will have to retake any classes that you have dropped or have failed.

You must never allow yourself to slip where you would have to drop a class. Dropping a class within a week of starting the semester may be all right because most universities will refund the tuition. Any longer and you still have to pay for the tuition. In addition, you will have to retake the class again. Now you would have paid twice for one class.

If you do drop classes or worse fail a class, your friends and other people will graduate ahead of you. You will be left behind. Your friends may even get the job that you wanted. In times of economic hardships, jobs are very hard to find.

Failing a class means, you lose that tuition cost and you have to retake the class. You also lower your grade point average, which is very difficult to bring back up. There are also some stipulations on the scholarships regarding maintaining a high grade point average. Do not forget, companies also look at grades when hiring new undergraduates.

Good study habits include reading constantly and highlighting key sentences or phrases. Try to be very close to the front in order to see what the professor is writing. This is essential in order to take great notes in the lecture halls. Start your homework immediately when you arrive at home. Make sure you are comfortable and have ample lighting for reading the textbooks.

Do not work to try to earn extra money during your regular semester classes. It will take up the time you need for studying and doing your homework. You will just be hindering your attempt to get the good grades you really need in college. This is not like going to grammar school or high school. You cannot take extra credits in order to try to make up for the bad grades. All the professors in the universities are on a timetable of lecturing and administering exams. They will not be able to give any second chances of taking a test again in order to get a better grade.

This is why you must stay focused on finishing your courses according to the university's schedule. You must remember that you are there only for four years. You need to keep pushing forward with your academic goals.

Do not take months of vacation during the summer off. You will be wasting the opportunity to acclimate yourself in the work environment. This is the time for you to get a summer job. You can earn extra money to help pay for your tuition not for your social activities. Remember you wanted adult treatment. You must be a responsible adult. Do not make any excuses of needing a break. Do not make excuses again saying you have to find yourself during your summer vacation. These excuses just lead to laziness and will not help you advance.

You need to prepare for your career and follow the advice. You need to be marketable by having the necessary skills and work experience. Remember, there are hundreds of new students upon graduation that you will be competing against for a professional position.

Do not be one of those people with an undergraduate degree but cannot get work in a company. You will not be able to support yourself. Do not settle for working in a coffee shop or pizza store. Do not become content in working in a small store doing easy work. You will not be happy and possibly quit. You are investing in your life and you must succeed. Your parents will not be able to take care of you throughout your adulthood.

Graduating College

You must get a professional job upon graduation. Do not take months off or worse a year off as a long vacation from your undergraduate study. The reason is there are many graduates that apply for the jobs you want. Never lapse into a non-caring teenager. You are an adult and must behave as one. It is your responsibility to follow through with your new life in a professional world.

In actuality, you must start looking for a job months before you graduate. Go to your councilor and get information on upcoming job fairs that will be held at the university you are attending. Apply to all the companies that are looking for people with your educational background. Always dress professionally in a suit when meeting the hiring manager for a company. Even if they are on your campus, dress accordingly. Go for interviews immediately when they become available.

Your college councilor will also help you create a professional resume. Be factual and include all extra curricular activities that you have. List all the summer jobs you have taken including your duties and responsibilities. This is where summer jobs in line with your undergraduate studies really help. All hiring companies look at this and use it as a criterion for hiring new undergraduates.

You must try to read about the company you will be interviewing. This will help you become more motivated about getting the job and it helps you see what kind of company it is. The hiring manager will also be impressed with the amount of research you have done about the company. It will make a lasting impression after you leave from the interview.

You must always prepare yourself when going to the interview. The reason is that hiring managers look for mature people to hire. Try to practice at home with a family member or a friend. Let them ask you questions that may come up in the interview. You can then practice your answers and get some critique on the answers. They will also be able to tell you where you can improve your answers. This exercise will make you better prepared for the interview. It will help lessen any nervousness that you may have going into the interviews.

4

Graduate Study

Value of Graduate Degree

A company that will pay for your graduate study is one of the main criteria you must use when looking for work. Go for your graduate study immediately when you do start working for a company that will pay the tuition costs. This degree is free for you to take. You must take advantage of this privilege being offered to everyone in the company.

It is not advisable to pursue a graduate degree if you are the one who will pay for the tuition. You still have student loans to pay from your undergraduate degree. These loans and the new ones you will incur from the graduate school will drain your savings. You may already have to pay rent, car loans, cellular phone bill and other utilities in order to support yourself.

You should never ask your parents to pay for your graduate degree. This is your own personal goal. However, do not go for a graduate degree on a full time basis. You need to start earning money in order to start paying off your student loans. There could be one extreme exception and that is if the university will waive all the tuition costs and possibly even let you stay on their campus apartment free. That is, you do not have to pay for the tuition and rental at all.

The graduate degree is a highly respected diploma and is acknowledged by all the U.S. companies. Having this on your resume will be extremely great. The graduate degree sets you apart from your colleagues and all the other employees in the company. It shows that you have discipline and perseverance. No doubt, you will be more intelligent after taking the course and you can command a higher salary.

Having the graduate degree gives you an extra edge over unfriendly people at work. You will know more about any business subjects and the proper way to address issues. You will notice that some of your colleague's suggestions may even seem mediocre at best. You will achieve these benefits from the graduate degree.

If you have not asked about the tuition reimbursement program during your interview, visit your company's human resource department and ask about it. You must do this before even applying to a university for graduate admission. Some companies may actually have certain approved universities in which the tuition will be reimbursed. This limits your choices of universities for the graduate study. You must then gather information from the approved universities regarding what graduate programs are available.

Types of Graduate Degrees

If you have engineering as your undergraduate, you can expand on your background by taking the Master of Science in Engineering. For example, I have a bachelor degree in Mechanical Engineering and the Master of Science in Mechanical Engineering (MSME). The MSME degree did look good in my resume as many interviewing managers praised it. Unfortunately, most of the manufacturing companies I worked for had no real applications for it. I never used all the knowledge I had gained in real life work projects.

One possible place where you could use the MSME degree would be a purely research facility where you will need to use the theories you have learned. You could even possibly work for the university's research department or a governmental agency.

One graduate class to pursue is the Master in Business Administration (MBA), especially if your undergraduate was in engineering or other science related field. This graduate degree will give you actual knowledge that you can use in your workplace. Just about all the U.S. companies have tuition programs for graduate study in the MBA.

In pursuing the MBA, you will have to decide what major to take. There are various types of MBA degree. Some of these are Accounting; Advertising; Business Ethics; Asian Business Studies; International Marketing; International Business; Economics; Telecommunications Management and Health Care. Some companies will only allow certain majors that employees can take for a full tuition reimbursement. Your company may require you to major in your current work position.

For example, I am in the mechanical engineering field and was given approval to take my MBA in Finance. This included the company paying my course books. However, after resigning and working for another company, my new workplace would not reimburse the tuition cost for my MBA because my major was in Finance. I therefore had to switch to Marketing as a major.

This is something you will have to be prepared to handle. You must be flexible to take a different major because of company policies. In any event, you must still go for your graduate degree. Your company will pay the tuition cost. All it takes is some dedication and time from you. Free education is being offered to anyone willing enough to sacrifice some time.

If you do not take this opportunity, other people in the company will take it. These people will get the degree and could possibly become your boss in a few years. The graduate degree is a great tool to use for advancing in your career. It will certainly look great on your resume when you start looking for another job.

An MBA will help broaden your work skills and business knowledge. It will open your mind on how things operate in the business world. This will make you even more valuable in your company. There are international programs you can pursue. If you love to travel, you could work for a company with international divisions. You could be visiting facilities overseas, such as the Philippines, China, or Japan. You may even be stationed overseas for months.

An MBA may even motivate you to start your own business. You will at least know what you would need to do and go about starting a company. The program teaches you how to protect yourself by forming an "S Corporation" so that you protect your personal assets. You learn the proper way to do cost analysis and to research any business projects.

Requirements

In pursuing an MBA, most universities will require you to take the Graduate Management Admission Test (GMAT). This test is similar to the American College Test (ACT) you had to take for your college entrance.

You must get a high GMAT score that is required by the university you want to attend. You must apply to at least three universities in case your first choice does not accept your application. Some prestigious universities require a formal recommendation from your current manager. Some universities even require you to write essays on their chosen topics.

There are study guidebooks for the GMAT available in bookstores and the library. You could even try the internet to purchase one. You must use this book and study the questions. There are sample tests that are very similar to the actual questions. You must sit down and time yourself in taking the whole test. There are the usual math, English and comprehensive sections. When the time is finished, grade yourself according to the instructions. This will show you how well you performed and what your grade would have been. Obviously, if the grade is low, you must study the appropriate subjects where you are weak.

You can also major in law for your graduate study. Some of the available majors are Patent Law; Corporate Law; Asian Legal System; Housing Law; Antitrust Law and Insurance Law. Even if you are an engineer or accountant, you can take Patent Law for your graduate degree. Again, make sure that your company will pay for your tuition costs.

For the law degree, you will have to take the Law School Admission Test (LSAT). This is the equivalent examination for the MBA's required GMAT. The LSAT happens four times a year in the U.S. The same advice for the GMAT applies here. You can buy an LSAT study guidebook and go through the test sections. You can also find information on the internet regarding the law graduate degree. Study hard for this also because it does require a lot of work.

If you do not have law as an undergraduate, you can still pursue becoming a lawyer. This will take you into an entirely different career path from your undergraduate degree. However, you must really have the desire to become a lawyer in pursuing this graduate program. You could then work either for a law firm or as a corporate lawyer. For example, I had to interact with the corporate patent lawyers when I was pursuing several patents. They were part of the staff at my old workplace.

For starters, you should introduce yourself to the university's pre-law advisor at the university you want to attend. The advisor can give you a more personal attention regarding any concerns and questions you have. Try to have a well-defined career goal before seeing the advisor. It will help you both in determining what you want to accomplish in your life. You may even find out that you do not wish to pursue law.

There are universities that also offer a combined program where you can receive an MBA and a Law Degree. The trade off is possibly two more years of graduate study. Therefore, after six years, you will graduate with both an MBA and Law Degree. This is especially good if you are extremely ambitious and can handle the possible six years of graduate study. The time to finish is obviously dependent on how many courses you might take per semester. It also depends on whether you drop any classes and take summer school.

One valuable advice in going for your graduate degree is not to even think whether you should even pursue one. Do exactly what is written here and go on automatic pilot. Sign up for the next GMAT examination that is scheduled within two to three months. This will give you enough time to prepare and study for it. It is also very close so that you do not have enough time to change your mind.

If the company has a preferred university for the tuition reimbursement, then apply to that university. Remember that many companies have agreements with some universities. If the company will reimburse your choice of university, then sign up with your choice.

You need to enroll immediately because you may feel that you need a break and want to do other fun things in your life. You may think that you would use too much time studying and may not have enough for your personal life. This is not true. In actuality, you would probably just be spending time watching T.V. every night. This hesitation will lead you to procrastinate on whether to continue studying after your undergraduate.

This is not the case. You will have time for some socializing and sports activities. You just need to manage your time accordingly. You will have some time during the weekends for hobbies and going to the movies. Remember you are only taking two classes per semester. Not like in undergraduate where you can have five to six classes.

You will learn how to prioritize your homework and house tasks to accomplish your graduate degree. This is part of living and is not new. You will find that in the classes that you are not alone. Everyone in the classroom is also sacrificing watching T.V. and going to many social events on the weekends. They are there learning with you instead of wasting time going to bars and drinking.

Some Benefits from an MBA

One great benefit with the MBA program is that it teaches you how to properly write an executive report and present it in front of people. It will help further your education in speaking in front of people and fielding questions. It helps you how to conduct meetings and to follow through with proper documentations. At times, you really need to do this in order to protect yourself from unscrupulous corporate politics.

Because you will only take two classes per semester in the graduate program, you will absorb more material. You have the chance to learn everything about the work environment and the tools to use. These business tools can be accounting procedures; break-even cost analysis; product costing and writing project reports.

You will learn about stocks and the stock market in the financial courses. You will know about the various ratios that a stock analyst uses on whether you should buy, sell or avoid a specific stock. The class will touch on the subject but not get into detail. You will understand the terminologies and the process of evaluating company stock. You will also learn about the relationship between bonds and interest rates. These are valuable lessons because you will see them often when you start enrolling in your company's 401k plan.

Other Issues with Graduate Degree

If you are unsure of what to do and regardless of your undergraduate degree, take the GMAT immediately and pursue the MBA in Marketing. Get all the paper work and tests out of the way while you still are thinking about the program. The first year for the MBA typically requires you to take basic courses which are common to many majors such Marketing and Finance. Moreover, you will be taking two courses per semester anyway. When you finally decide what you want as a major, you can easily switch your program. The main message is to keep advancing yourself without thinking about it.

Pursuing a doctorate degree will be entirely up to you. If you have a great desire to teach at university or become a researcher, then this degree will help you. Many companies do not require you to have a doctorate degree. In fact, you may become over qualified for a company where you want to work.

There will be times when you may want to quit and discontinue your graduate degree. You could be almost halfway done with the courses and doubt whether it was a good idea to pursue your degree. You may become impatient and want to do other things in your life. You may become discouraged and that it is taking too long to get your degree.

However, do not get discouraged. The four years will go by so quickly you will not even notice it. You have other activities you need to accomplish during your graduate study. You should be saving your money and budgeting yourself for a house you will have to purchase. Your workplace may also have recreational activities such as a volleyball league or basketball league you could join every summer. Things like this will help you pass the time.

Some of your friends or other people may discourage you from going for your graduate degree. They may not be looking out for your best interest. They may be jealous of what you are accomplishing and may not want you to succeed. Do not listen to them. You must get your graduate degree and finish what you have started.

There are many people who do want to pursue their graduate study in the MBA program. However, the majority of them wait until they are in their thirties or older. For some, this is harder to accomplish because they already have a set schedule and lifestyle. They may have a family of their own including children that will need a lot of attention.

At least, you are still young coming out of the undergraduate program and have a more time. It will be easier for you also since you still remember many pertinent courses in your undergraduate study that you will need in the graduate program. In addition, you still have your study habits that are very essential in the program.

5

Work Environment

Work Advice and Corporate Culture

When you are in a work environment, perform all your appointed tasks in a professional manner. Respect your manager and do exactly the tasks he had given to you. Perform the tasks as described in the job description and beyond it when possible. You must learn the company's systems and procedures by heart. Do all the medial work, all the paper chasing as much as possible. This method will help you learn the ins and outs of your department as well as the other departments.

Learn how to fill all the forms in your department. This will actually make your work easier because you are removing bottlenecks in paper work for you. You will know which persons from each department must sign and approve the paper work you need to accomplish your tasks. By doing this, you can really excel in your career.

Speak up clearly when participating in a meeting and more importantly when doing a presentation. Be concise in discussing issues with your manager and colleagues. You must think through the issues before giving your recommendations. When you finally give your recommendations, give it with great convictions.

Growing up in your parent's home where your native tongue is spoken will affect your speech patterns. It will give you an accent that is usually associated with your native dialect. In order to deal with this, you must take up some speech classes. Practice speaking properly so that your accent is not as prevalent. Expand your vocabulary and enunciate each syllable. Perform this exercise repeatedly and soon it will be automatic. This will help you gain more confidence in all your presentations.

Remember that you are new in the company and you do not know how your colleagues and other employees interact with each other. You do not know which people are friends with each other. You do not know which people dislike each other. You need to be quiet in the first few months at work. Learn which people you can trust and which ones may discredit you. This does not mean to totally distrust everybody and start fights. You must learn how to read and evaluate people.

Look at the clothes they wear and observe their business ethics. Study very carefully how they treat other people, especially people close to your ethnicity. You will quickly learn which people are still harboring discriminatory feelings. Try very hard to stay away from these prejudiced people. There will be times when this will be very difficult especially if you work directly with them. If this is the case, be very professional and document everything that you do. These include meeting notes, projects and sometimes conversations. With conversations, you can send a follow up memo or email which covers the issues and action items.

You must find out what is the corporate culture in the company. The managers and executives may run things in a relaxed manner. There could be very little professionalism in the company. People may not be documenting meetings and reports. Everyone may be doing his or her jobs mostly by verbal communications.

This type of culture can be dangerous for you. If something goes wrong in your department, people target you as the source of the problem. You could be very innocent but if there were no documentation, you will not be able to defend yourself properly. It will be the words of other people against yours. Your colleagues who have been with the company for a long time will band together to protect each other. However, you will not be included because you are the new employee. You must never get into this type of situation.

On the other hand, the company could be very strict in professionalism. Everybody could be using computers constantly to email and document meetings. You will fill out many in order to finish your job. The best thing is to know the procedures and go with the flow in the company.

You must try to have a friend with you when you need to discuss something important with any prejudiced people. This is a very important tactic, especially if one of them is your supervisor. Your friend will automatically be a witness to these types of meeting. It is one way of giving yourself insurance in case there is a plot to discredit your work. This method also dissuades any idea of harassment that may be forming.

Be careful of other people who will treat you in a derogatory manner. They will report any miniscule error that you may have done. The error may be so insignificant but your discriminating colleagues will blow it out of proportion. We still live in world where discrimination is alive in the workplace. You must take every precaution in dealing and handling these people. Never ever, challenge or provoke them. You are too new and you will not have any true friend that will be able to help you. You are on your own and must still learn whom you can trust.

Clothing Attire

Always wear clothing according to the company's dress code. If you are in the professional field, wear appropriate business suits or dress depending if you are a male or female. Do not wear something that is flashy or too trendy. People will view you as a wild person. Just wear conventional and traditional work clothing. Your colleagues will perceive you as a professional.

Do not propagate stereotypes of your cultural background and profession. You will be validating these untrue behaviors. Do not wear short sleeve shirts and ties together during the summer. Wear a long sleeved shirt and roll up the sleeves because this looks much nicer. Wear loose fitting cotton shirts that allow air to flow freely. If you need glasses, wear a nice wire frame that fits your facial features. Ask advice the sales person for advice on which frames look good on you.

For both male and female, dark suit colors would be good. These could be navy blue or dark gray or even black. These colors are easier to match for the men with the light colored shirts and ties. The same is true for women but with a nice light colored blouse. Even if many of your colleagues do not wear nice business clothes, you can wear it. For more ideas, buy some magazines that advertise clothes for professional males and females. You can also ask for advice from reputable stores. They will be more than happy to give suggestions.

You may even want to buy at least one custom made suit. The prices are just about the same as that for off the rack suits. The main difference is that the custom suit will fit you perfectly and is very comfortable to wear. You can pick your own fabric pattern, jacket and pant style. The jacket can be single or double-breasted while the pants can be straight or pleated. It is entirely up to your taste which features you choose. Overall, you will look sharper in a custom suit because of the better fit.

Distractions

Develop good work ethics as you go along on your career. You must exhibit good behavior and manners in your workplace. Be courteous to people and address them properly. Try not to interrupt people when they are speaking. You will also get a chance to speak. Give your answers objectively and try to make them logical. You do not want to blurt out things during a conversation.

You must have a career goal in your job. You should also identify the necessary skills needed to meet your career goals. These could be taking work-sponsored seminars or actually going for your graduate study. Stay focused on this path as you go about your work.

You must stay away from petty office fights and politics. There usually are no winners. You must always turn the other cheek. Let the people involved with the politics disagree among them. Do not get frustrated over trivial things. Do not get distracted with stress from the workload and pressures. It will interfere with your work and career path. You must stay focused on your career goals.

One of the worst distractions in the workplace can be an office romance. Try very hard not to date anyone from work. There is truth in the saying you hear from other people regarding office dating. You know from experiences in a social gathering that it is very uncomfortable to see someone you had dated.

Remember the unpleasant feeling and multiply it by a hundred times. You will be seeing the person you dated at work possibly everyday. The worst scenario could be you and the person you dated work in the same department. There could be hard feelings that will make one of you take revenge on the other. Any small mistakes that may happen between you two at work can lead to arguments.

Another bad thing that can happen is that the person will eventually talk badly about you. The person can possibly spread unfounded rumors about you. This is nothing new. This usually happens in an office romance and it can happen to you. It will affect how you perform at work and at graduate school if you are in a program.

There are many men or women you can meet outside the workplace. You will find many opportunities to become intimate with them. You will have all the time in the world for this. Do not use the workplace to find someone for you to date. Many things can go wrong. It will be better for you to go dancing in a nightclub with friends from school.

Personal Goals

You must have a monetary goal also. You must plan for your future and early retirement. Working solely for a company these days is not the only way you can plan for your future. Save as much money as you can. Allocate some money for your recreation and vacation. Nevertheless, do not spend too much money.

Sign up for the 401K plan with your employer. However, you must contribute only the minimum percentage, which the employer will match. This percentage will be different for every company. For example, one company may require a minimum two percent before it matches fifty cents for every one dollar you contribute.

When you do accept a position in a manufacturing or technology oriented company, you are required to sign forms that deal specifically with innovation and invention. This form states that any innovation you create will be the property of the company when it pursues the patent. Your name will be on the patent but that is all. All the monetary benefits go directly to the company. There is no royalty or any amount of monetary compensation given to you. This includes stocks, stock options or any other type of monetary instrument.

Go ahead and pursue a patent for the company but do it under special conditions. If someone has already started the patent application, go ahead and get your name included. If somebody else's product idea was submitted for a patent, again join in and get your name included. However, do not improve the idea any further. The reason is you can pursue a new patent containing your improvement.

Put a lot of effort in writing the patent and filling the forms. Get all the experience in the proper procedure for writing a patent and submitting it to the company's patent lawyer. You will need these skills later when you do want to pursue an invention on your own.

Do not volunteer any brilliant product idea that you may have conceived. You will not get any royalties or form of payment. This includes any software product you may develop. Do not disclose your potential invention to your colleagues, friends or even family members. The idea may leak out to someone else. They can then apply for the patent. What you need to do is to document your idea in your home personal computer or even pieces of paper. Develop your idea properly and try to design it so that it can be manufactured easily.

If you can make prototypes, do make it. Even the crudest prototypes are enough to help convey the idea. Write up the patent forms, create drawings and document your claims with a signature. Set these documents aside for later submission to the United States Patent and Trademark Office (USPTO).

As for a software idea, you must apply for the copyright protection with the USPTO. All the information you need for protection is contained in the website. The main thing to remember is to use only your own personal computer and printer. If you do not have one, then it is time for you to get one. You can get a very basic computer for very little money these days. Do not use your company's computers and other resources. The company can lay claim to your idea.

Pursuing a patent is one type of backup plan for your future. Other ones are very basic. Save as much money as you can. Do not start buying very expensive fast cars just to impress the opposite sex or for status symbol. You will be draining your cash into maintaining the car. Besides, you cannot take a car into a bar and impress anyone. The best thing you can do is be yourself and attract someone from a good first impression.

You must also pursue your graduate degree as soon as possible once you start working. Just about all the companies will pay for your graduate tuition. You must take advantage of this free education, which will help further your career. You will learn how to better yourself and speak the business language.

The graduate degree will help you in many ways. It will help you get ahead in your current company should you still be there. The degree will also make you more marketable when you want to leave your company. It gives your resume a more substantial content other than past tasks described.

Make owning a house one of your goals. Start with a small single home. Townhouses and condominiums are also great starts in owning a home. They can be more affordable depending on the size and location. One thing to keep in mind is you should not keep paying rent, which can reach up to a thousand dollars per month. This is about how much you would pay for a mortgage, depending on the type and cost of house. The main difference is that you are building equity with the mortgage whereas the rental cost is gone forever. You are giving to a stranger thousands of dollars, which you will never get back.

Dealing with Attitudes

You must have a working resume ready at all times while you are working. Even if you just received your undergraduate degree, you must create one at home and update it every year. There will be a time when you will need your resume in times of emergency. In these days and time, there are no more secure jobs. You must accept the fact that you will be changing jobs many times.

Never ever, trust any companies no matter how profitable they appear. Remember the large corporations you see in the news where the top executives have embezzled millions of dollars. Do not trust your employer totally. You will never know when your company may layoff people due to sudden economic downturns. You could be part of the crowd that will be laid off because of corporate mismanagement.

You could also be at the same level in the company for years and not be promoted. The managers may hold you back because of your high efficiency. They could be afraid that you will be promoted above them. On the other hand, there could be just plain discrimination in all the managers and they do not want to see an Asian advance. You must be prepared for the worst at all times.

There may even be some restructuring in your department due to downsizing. Sometimes your departmental manager or vice president is fired. Be very careful of any new hired executives. All these people will always bring their friends and old colleagues into the company. These people will evaluate every person in your department and systematically eliminate them. They will do this by any means and justify it by showing how the targeted employees' inefficiency contributed to the company's downturn. They need to clean the department to make room for their friends and colleagues.

Once these new executives have hired their friends, you must watch yourself at all times. You must really start looking for a new job because you could eventually be the next person to be laid-off or fired. These are the facts of corporate life for Asians and other minorities.

It is also acceptable to talk to recruiters in order to keep yourself updated on the current job market. Even though you are not searching for a new job, it does not hurt to learn if another company may want to hire you. Go ahead and make an appointment for the interview since they are interested in your background and skills. Consider this step as your own personal promotion to yourself. Why wait for your own current employer to reward you with a promotion when you can secure a new job. You can also increase your salary should the new potential company hire you.

Knowing that you have a working resume also provides a peace of mind. You will also experience managers that will be overbearing and unreasonable to you. Remember, these are all just people with regular human behaviors and feelings. These managers may see something in you that they do not like or appreciate. They may see colors because of your cultural background. If these things happen, these managers will be on your case all the time.

You must document your important work properly. Use the company email to forward any memos, reports, or minutes. Make sure you copy pertinent colleagues whenever possible. Do not send the email to just one person. You must copy some other people as future witnesses. Also, save the sent email copy into an archive folder. Never delete these files until you are ready. These emails are just one form of documenting your important work.

You must write up formal reports whenever possible. Save all these works, the emails and all the associated data in diskettes. Take the diskettes home for archiving purposes. When you are absolutely done with the files, you can always erase them and reuse the diskettes.

These bad managers will find any excuse to give you a hard time and make your job very difficult to do. They will discredit you and give you bad reviews that are unfounded. You will become a marked target. Be very careful with whom you talk to in the company. Even if you make a small comment about your job or the company, it will eventually make its way to your manager. Your manager will take this opportunity and will direct your comment against you.

The fortunate thing is that you are just dealing with one manager in the instance above. However, all companies have groups of people that will protect each other. Remember this very important point. There is a thing called "good old boys club" in companies. These people could be old timers, college friends, or worst, friends who share the same views about foreigners. These people will always look out for each other even though they are doing the wrong things.

They have gone through many good and bad situations in the company that created certain camaraderie with each other. Maybe one of them had saved someone else from being embarrassed in a meeting. Someone could have covered up a mistake for his friend. Sometimes the most basic truth is that they are protecting each other's job. They would rather work with each other even if one of them were incompetent.

Because you have not been through this with any of them, you are an outsider. Obviously, you will not be trusted fully and will be under scrutiny. The worst thing that can happen is that you get a manager that has something against you. It could be your racial background, religion, or just the way you look. There really is no way of knowing what really irritates a manager about employees. This is something that you will have to determine for yourself regarding your manager's attitude towards you.

There are things that you can do to help you learn about a company's corporate culture. Look at how the managers treat other foreigners. Look around the prospective company and make sure there are other minority employees. Preferably, there should be other Asians or other ethnic background working in the company. Especially, there should be Asian managers in various departments such as Accounting, Human Resource and Purchasing. See if the other managers give these Asian managers the proper respect and professionalism.

You must be alert at all times. This is most important when you go for interviews. Observe the people working in the company. You can tell if they are happy there by their tone of voice. Another way to tell is if the people greet you warmly. Do not be afraid to ask them questions. Find out how they really like the company and even the manager.

The main thing to remember in the work environment is to stay out of trouble. Avoid confrontations with managers, colleagues and other people in the company. One way or another, you will be the one that will get into trouble. If someone is purposely creating a bad situation with you, end it quickly and quietly. Do this by saying you have a very important meeting to attend or that you have a very important personal phone call to make. Be very creative and quick. Turn around and start walking away. Never show your anger no matter how much you want to show it.

You must always be passive in any conversations in the company. Do not let the managers and colleagues know what you are thinking at all times. This will be one of your advantages. This way they will not know what you may do next in your career.

In some conversations, it will be best if you just say the obvious things. This way, your manager or colleagues cannot dispute you. They cannot say anything bad about your comments. You will not experience pressure into explaining your comments and finally defending it. You must remember there are many managers who will always look down upon Asians and other minorities. There are still managers who will distrust any type of ethnic group. This is an unpleasant fact, which you must endure as long as you work for a corporation.

Regardless of what company you work for, hold your head up high. You must have an air of dignity about yourself. Show how proud you are of your culture and never show any disrespect of anyone. You must be a role model for your colleagues and everyone else at work. Remember that you are the one who will always do the right things and know that you are doing the right things. This way you will never doubt yourself whether you have made the right decisions in your workplace.

6

Investments

Single Person Living with Parents

Although you may be in your twenties, it is acceptable in your Asian culture to live with your parents for some more years. This will help you save money while you work in a company. Yes, you may have to pay rent to help your parents, but this amount is small compared to renting an actual apartment. You must remember that your parents raised you and took care of you when you were sick. They will continue to help you as you establish yourself in the business world. They know how hard it would be for you to save money because of all the bills you will start to pay.

You might think that having a roommate will help you save some more money. This may not be the case. Apartment rental costs could still be very expensive because of its location. You may not be able to save money as you had planned. The reason is that you will still incur other expenses once you live on your own and start working.

There are heating, water and phone bills that will have to be paid. You will realize that the average costs for gas heat is about $100 while phone bills can average about $50 to $80 depending on your usage. This phone bill does not include cellular phone bills. Remember that these days the gas bills usually go up every year.

Owning a House

Once you have saved enough money, then you are ready for real estate. This will be the most important investment in your life. Provided you already know you will not be moving around too much, then you must really plan to buy a house. You can buy a small ranch style dwelling, a townhouse or even a condominium.

The townhouse and condominium usually do not cost as much depending on the size and location.

This is where it counts that you maintain a good credit rating and a steady job. Always maintain a low balance on your credit card so that you can pay it all the following month. This also holds true for any utility and car payments that you have in your name. You need this good credit rating in order to get you mortgage loan approved.

You must own a home for at least three reasons. The first one is that real estate goes up in value. Secondly, you get a tax shelter on your income. Thirdly, you do get back the money as equity on the monthly mortgage payments. Instead of paying hundreds of dollars rent in an apartment, you can be using that money into a mortgage payment. Think about it. You will never recover your rental money.

Stay in your house and always try to maintain its appearance and structure. You need to tuck point the bricks and replace the roof when it becomes necessary. You do not want any water intrusion going through the walls and ceiling during a rainstorm. Always check the walls and ceiling during a storm to make sure there are no leaks. If you see any small discoloration in the paint, then there is usually a water leak happening. You must fix the leak immediately and not let it get worse. Look under contractors in the phone book and get at least three quotes. When you find someone good, you can always call him or her back for future work.

Maintain your water heater, air conditioner and heater at every year. Sign up with local repair shops where you can insure your air conditioner, heater, washer and dryers. Good repair shops want to come once a year to clean up the air conditioner and heater free. They want to perform preventive maintenance on your equipment so that they will not break down during the season you need them most. All these things contribute to the appreciation of your home and therefore, the money you put into the house is not lost.

You must save money by buying generic inexpensive types dinner plates, pots and pans. You should buy a small eating table and chair. Shop around and buy things at different times. For example, buy your plate sets one month, cookware the next month, and dining table the next month. You do not have to buy them all at the same time. This method also spreads out your credit card payment so can easily pay it all up every month. By doing this, you avoid paying the high interest rate charge. You should also sign up for a store's credit card that offers zero percent financing for a year when you do need to by something expensive there. Just be sure to pay it all off before the expiration date.

One of the great things you can do is try to get kitchenware, dining and living room furniture hand downs from your family members. Ask around your family for old tables, chairs, sofas and other home furnishings. Do not worry because these will not be your final furniture. Keep in mind that you do not overload your home with too many things. It will be easier for you to move furniture around when you start upgrading your house.

If you do not need a new television and DVD player, do not buy one yet. Hold off in buying many expensive electronic toys. Again, you can save money by using your old one from your parent's house. Another thing you can do to save money is to use the free internet web servers if you really have to browse the internet. You may even find an internet café to be more affordable, depending on how often you need it. You should no subscribe to any cable T.V. for your entertainment. The monthly fees just does not justify having it. You are better off in renting the movies. These are luxury items that you do not necessarily need. The main point is to minimize your cash out flow, which are your expenses.

Sometimes it is even better if you keep eating out at reasonable restaurants instead of cooking at home. The reason is when you cook for one person you will eat leftovers for a few days. In addition, you use up electric, water and gas costs to prepare your food. In addition, if you do not finish the leftovers, you end up throwing the food away. You must remember also that the food is getting older as the days go by. You could end up getting sick from eating the old food.

Remodeling Your Home

When you are comfortable enough and have enough money, you can delve more into the real estate investment. You can buy a second house, townhouse or condominium. However, you must purchase what you can afford without stretching your money too thinly. Make sure that you will have enough cash in your bank account to cover the extra expenses in the other house. The reason is that you may not have a renter right away. On the other hand, if you want to sell the house, it may take up to a year. You must make sure that you can cover the mortgages and utilities.

You can buy a cheap house that you can remodel. When you do start this investment, you must do it with a budget. Write down all the costs you will have to pay. Make sure you estimate the jobs very carefully and actually plan to add another 50% of the cost to your initial budget. It is very typical that you will go over the budget whenever you do a major house-remodeling project.

There are usually hidden costs and other surprises as you slowly tear down and rebuild a house. This could range from rerouting electrical wirings to replacing the heater. Other things that can drain your money are the actual contractors you use. The surprises that you come across will extend the labor time, which adds up very fast. Because the extra work is not in the original contract, they will charge you overtime.

You must make sure that you write down the exact work you want done by the various contractors you hire. Use the same lists when you start looking for various quotes. This will help you track the progress and costs. You want to make sure they do accomplish the work.

You must at least obtain three quotes from different contractors to get an idea of how much you should really spend. Some contractors will overcharge while others will be just perfect. Take your time and ask around if you need advice on which contractors to use.

Once your new house is completed, you can then rent it out to possibly college students or people who just moved into the city. The rental cost will help pay for the extra mortgage you acquired. Otherwise, you could sell the house outright and take the profits. You can then use the profits for the next house project if you wish.

Owning a Car

Someday you will eventually buy a car. You will definitely need a car if you are working somewhere in the suburbs. The reason is that there usually is no public transportation. You will need a car in order to get around. You must realize that buying a car is not an investment. However, it is such an expensive item that you must know what to do.

Everyone knows that automobiles depreciate the moment it leaves the dealership. You will not recover your money from buying any car. Never justify buying an expensive car as an investment that you would then sell years later for a profit. The car will just get old and possibly be in an accident. Yes, face the fact that you will eventually get into an accident even if you are a safe driver. You will not get any return on your investment on the car.

Owning a car is one of the biggest responsibilities you will undertake. You will need to maintain the car in good working condition to ensure safe driving on the highway and city streets. You would not want to become stranded on an interstate highway miles away from home.

You will need oil and oil filters changed periodically around every 2,500 miles. Depending on your driving habits, you will need car repairs as the mileage adds up. There are also your weekly fuel costs for work and leisure. You must have car insurance, which is the law.

You can save money on buying a car by getting a nice inexpensive reliable one. Do not buy a sports car, which will have a very low gas mileage. The insurance cost will be higher for a sports car especially for a foreign one. Your new driver status does not help either. The car maintenance is also much higher for the foreign sport cars. Keep this in mind when you are shopping for cars.

Buy a good reliable mid size car with a high gas mileage rating. Shop around and visit many dealers. Ask many questions and do not be swayed easily by car salespersons. Before you go looking for a car, figure out the monthly car payments you would have to pay. If you can, do this in a spreadsheet. Include a realistic interest rate and taxes. The result will give you a benchmark on what you can afford.

In fact, create another spreadsheet that will have your cash flow in and cash flow out. Include all the daily, weekly, monthly and yearly expenses that you experience. For example, include your daily food cost for the whole week. You can convert this easily to a monthly figure. Other items you must include are hair care costs; rental cost; food, air fare and hotel vacation costs; clothing costs; car fuel cost; car insurance cost; car payments; desired monthly savings for your future house purchase. The result will show your monthly final savings from your current salary. It will show how much you can really afford in monthly car payments and maintenance.

With these two spreadsheets, you can go into a car dealer with high confidence on what you can afford. For example, tell them up front that you want your final monthly payment to be $180. Let them work out all the other numbers in the back office. They can give you this figure by lowering the price, interest rate and by increasing the loan's number of years.

Once you have purchased a car, try to keep it for as long as you can. This really depends on how many miles per day you will drive. For example, if you are going to average 60 miles per day, you may want to keep it until you have over 100,000 miles on it. However, this will really depend on what car you own.

When you are ready, contribute to your company's 401K Plan. Sign up for the minimum percentage contribution where your company matches some dollar amount. Do not contribute the maximum amount right away. This will help you accumulate cash into your saving account. You may still need to generate enough savings first which you can use in time of emergencies.

Hiring a Financial Planner

Once you have settled down with your work, car payments and other expenses you will have a better handle on your cash flows. Once you have this, then you must sign up with a reputable financial planner. Try to use a large company. There are many out there but be careful. Ask around and read their performance statements.

The financial planner will help you manage your money even more. Your planner will develop a portfolio according to your work status. You will plan your retirement age and how much money you would need to achieve that goal. It will include how much money you need to save for house and car. Be assured that this must be your first investment options because it is more conservative. It forces you to start saving money while allowing you an allowance for other investment opportunities on your own. These other investments will be higher risks with the exceptions of the real estate investment and graduate study.

Pursuing a Graduate Degree

Pursue your graduate study, such as Masters in Business Administration (MBA), immediately once you start working. Your workplace will pay for the tuition costs and various textbooks. You must take advantage of this privilege that is offered free. Yes, this is a high privilege in this country but not too many people use it. It will only take a few years, which will go by quickly. While you are attending graduate school, you can plan your other types of investments. You must do this for your future.

If you do pursue an MBA, you can major in Marketing, which will greatly help your other investment ideas. You can apply the business knowledge in starting possible companies such as restaurants, hair salons or anything that you really love to do. Remember that you will get the degree free. The important asset you are using is your free time in pursuing the MBA. Therefore, never give up and make a point to finish your graduate degree.

Getting the graduate degree will make you more valuable to your employer. They should promote you and give you a higher pay. If your employer does not give you these rewards, then you must start looking around for a new job. Always other companies will want to hire you for your experience and skills.

Investing in Yourself

You must invest in yourself. Start your own company. Go into ventures that you can achieve with your limited resources. If you already have a computer, write a book or an article for a magazine. The articles could be funny accounts from a vacation or family holiday gathering. Alternatively, if you have a creative and artistic mind, you could develop web sites for people or small businesses. You would need a web designer program and possibly a digital camera.

You can take lessons in cooking and work in a restaurant until you have learned the business. After a few years, you can then open your own restaurant or diner. Find out your best interest and hobbies. Find your best ability and nurture it. These are better types of investments. Remember that you want your investments to appreciate and give a good solid return.

It is not advisable to buy a franchise store. Some of these require you to pay a start up fee ranging up to $25,000. You will also be required to pay an annual fee and for training all the employees. All these are in the first year and you have not even started producing or making money yet.

Patents are another way to invest if your goal is to make income from them. Whether you are an engineer, medical doctor, machine operator or bank clerk, you can think of a product idea that could be marketable. Write down your ideas and develop these, if possible, into working prototypes. Do all the research yourself and at your home. Use only your personal computer, printer and camera. Do not use your company's assets because they could lay claim to your invention. Once you feel confident in your ideas, you can pursue a patent application.

The best thing is to employ a reputable agency that will take care of the patent application and perform the marketing plan. This is highly suggested because the agency has the necessary distribution contacts and potential companies that will purchase the license rights. They will also take care of the legal aspects in obtaining the patents and negotiate the royalty payments to you.

Another simple investment you can do is to protect any type of software improvements or ideas you may have. Just like with the patents, do not just hand over your original software idea to your workplace. The company will claim your idea. You can apply for a copyright to protect your idea and then market it or license it to a major corporation. The same advices for the patents apply here. Do not use your company's resources in order to create your unique software. You do not want your company to lay claim to all your hard work, which could bring in millions of dollars in revenue.

Although the majority of ideas listed above do not require a lot of cash outlay, you must always have enough cash in your bank account for credible investment opportunities. You also need this cash reserve in cases of personal emergencies.

When you do pursue some of the investment ideas, do not get distracted from your efforts. You must create a schedule with definite target dates for certain milestones pointing towards your main goal of financial success. Talk to other people if you need some push and motivation along the way. Pace yourself so that you do not become overworked. However, always remember that you must put forth the effort. You will have to sacrifice many things such as social events in order to succeed.

Non-Investment Items

There are things that some people consider investments but are not in reality. Some of the items you should not buy as investments are: stamps and coins; jewelries; paintings and antique furniture. Do not consider these as investments but as hobbies. You should really try to base your investment decision on ideas that will yield a real return on your investment, including the transaction fees. The investments should also be easy to liquidate when you really need the money.

There are no get rich quick schemes. If such a thing exists, the people offering the schemes should be millionaires already. If these so-called investments yielded high returns, then why would they need your money? Do not participate in any pyramid-structured activities. You will just waste your money on the initiation fees and cash participation.

Do not sign up for time-sharing vacations and condominiums. Your allocated time to use these places is lost every year if you do not use the package or place. You have just thrown away your vacation money. You are not saving any money for your vacations. There are so many competitive vacation packages offered by travel agencies and even the airlines. You can see vacation packages advertised on T.V. and in the newspapers. Read each one carefully and compare prices.

Do not freely give away your hard-earned money to family members and friends offering any type of investment opportunity. They may present you with cash flows on a piece of paper but that is all. Anybody can fabricate an income statement showing high returns. Many of these are frauds require large sums of cash up front. Do not buy from these people no matter how well you know them. Unfortunately, they have already been conned and need to be re-educated.

7

Patents

Personal Patents

Patents give legal protection on any ideas or inventions that you may have developed. It will give you protection from other people or companies in using your invention without your approval. Usually, you can apply for a design patent or a utility patent. The design patent protects the look of your invention while the utility patent protects the usage of your invention.

Part of a patent submission requires a cursory patent search to help ensure the idea is something worthwhile to pursue. You can do this with your home computer by going into the internet. The United States Patent and Trademark Office (USPTO) is the governmental agency that can provide all the information you need to know regarding patents and applying for patents. You must look into their website www.uspto.gov to learn more about the different types of patents. You can easily view this free public resource. The site also contains the patent submission fees and the necessary forms you will need. You can get further help by calling the phone number in the web site.

You can also perform your own patent searches regarding any ideas that you have. You must do this before actually pursuing a patent. You will see if your product idea has already been patented, thus saving you time and money.

Using your own personal computer cannot be stressed enough. It is a way of proving that you created your invention at home and not through your workplace. It shows that you created your invention using personal equipment and personal time. Never ever, use your company's computer, copying machine and fax machines to document and prepare your patent application. You should not have your invention show at your work place. If it does show up, then the company can lay claim to the invention. You will lose all your valuable work to your company.

Although you are not supposed to market anything related to your line of work, it is advisable to document the ideas so that you can pursue them after a job change. In fact, look at some of the company startups made by former employees. These people are not in jail and are doing lucratively.

There are several things to keep in mind. If you just want a patent under your name and not make any profit from it, then you may as well just get one with your current employer. Should you want to make money from the invention, then the patent application is the first step. There are several ways to make a profit from the invention.

You can pursue the patent on your own and pay for all the patent fees to the U.S. government. There is also the matter of paying the patent lawyer that will have to be hired. The USPTO requires a specific patent lawyer in order to process the patent application. The lawyers will charge you on an hourly basis and this can get very expensive. This will definitely cost thousands of dollars in just getting a patent. You must exercise great care in choosing the right patent lawyer. Remember, this is just for a patent application for now. The patent office will review the application and with luck approve it.

If everything goes very well, it takes about a year to receive the "patent pending" wording. With the "patent pending" label, you can safely show your product to the public for marketing or manufacturing reasons.

Please keep in mind the ultimate reasons for pursuing a patent for a new product idea and invention. You should view the patent as an investment instrument where you can receive a return. You must never pursue a patent where your employer would own it and you where you would never see a dime from all the profits it brings. An awarded patent can be a means for becoming independently wealthy and not work for anybody else, ever.

When you have received the "patent pending" label, you can take several paths. Be forewarned that all the paths will have costs associated with them. Some of the paths will be very expensive and will require a lot of work.

Forming a Company

If income is the motivating factor from the invention, you must incorporate yourself. An "S Corporation" is the most sensible in the beginning. This will separate personal assets such as your house, personal savings and wages. You are protecting your personal assets from lawsuits that may arise from the invention or product.

You can definitely pursue the patent but you will need enough cash to cover the various costs along the way. Some people may wait to try to raise enough cash. However, if the wait is too long, the opportunity can become smaller and smaller. As time goes by, anyone can and will become complacent or even lazy and not pursue the invention. This is the costliest mistake that anybody can make. Your opportunity to make a sizeable income from the product will disappear and can transfer to another individual or company.

A possible suggestion is for you is to take a business partner who will share the costs, labor and profits exactly fifty percent. For example, I have exactly done this and verbalized that we would share the profits exactly in half no matter who comes up with the other product ideas and inventions. This eliminates any ratio calculations and other small petty issues. By doing this, we are very free to invent and formalize other product ideas and not worry about who is getting the credits or doing work. The main thing that really counts is that the product is successful and we are equally sharing the monetary profits.

Other people have suggested taking on investment firms but this also requires a lot of work. You would then be subject to group approvals before you can even do anything. Your actual profit share will be smaller in a venture. What happens is that the inventor will not get his due share even though the product was totally his idea.

The associated costs in creating a product include patent costs, manufacturing costs, packaging costs, distribution costs, inventory costs, sales and marketing costs. Nobody should really start making the product unless he knows or already have a store contact that will put the product on the shelf for sale. Many stores may not even buy the product for sale.

For example, look at an invention of a small plastic part, which will require a plastic injection mold to make it. The mold would have to be purchased and this could cost $25,000 to $40,000 depending on the size. Once the mold has been purchased, then the parts would have to be bought and properly packaged. The purchased goods will then have to be shelved somewhere and brought to a store for sale. This means you will need some cash to pay for the products and for the storage facility.

Do not forget that you would have to find stores that will allow the product to be placed on their shelves. What this means is that you would have to do some old fashion legwork and go door to door looking for a buyer. You also will need actual consumers to buy the products.

When you do think of something, find someone you can trust and who will share in doing some of the legwork. It is be better to find someone outside of work. You would not want to ask your colleague. The reason is that the person may disclose the idea to the executives to advance in the company.

Combine your assets together such as personal computer, printer, fax machine, paper, and other home office equipment. You do not need to spend a lot of money in trying to set up a home office environment. You can subscribe to the free internet service providers around you area. You do not need to pay an expensive monthly fee in order to retrieve information from the internet. However, never ever transmit your product idea through the internet. Somebody can always find it and claim it.

You can also go to an internet café where it is very inexpensive. However, make sure that you do not work on your product idea using the internet café's computer. Your product idea may become stored in their computer and this all that is required for you to lose ownership. Someone can find it and quickly submit it to a company. You must be very protective of your product idea. In fact, never even talk about it over the telephone and cellular phone. Do not even fax the sketch or product description. Someone can intercept the fax steal your idea. You must deal with the attorneys and agencies through the mail.

This is your chance to show your creativity and perseverance by pursuing a personal patent. Just make sure that the product idea is marketable and that you must feel very comfortable with it. If there is any doubt about the idea, do not pursue it. You may just need to revise it, which can be easily done. However, you may have to dismiss an idea if you cannot improve it. This is okay to do because it gives you another opportunity to create something else. At least you will not waste your hard-earned money on something that may not yield any income.

Product Agencies

All these costs can be overwhelming especially if you carry all the burdens. However, do not be discouraged. There are other ways to try to make a profit from the patent without having to put up all the costs.

There are agencies that can be contracted who will provide the patent search and patent application for the inventor. They will also provide the necessary marketing and contract negotiations with prospective customers. With this method, there is a fee but which already includes the lawyer fees for the patent search and application. All that you would need to provide is a small written description of the invention.

The agency will provide the appropriate analysis on how much the invention could be sold in the market. The analysis will include the U.S. market share and target markets. They will also have the necessary contacts on potential companies that may want to purchase the license agreements from the inventor. The idea behind this is to license the acquired patent and to receive yearly royalties, hopefully for the life of the patent. There is a choice on collecting a lump sum of money or receiving pure royalties. Usually, the best thing to do would be to collect on the royalties alone.

A good reliable agency will also comment on the invention and will give good advice. They will actually reject ideas that are not marketable. You should pursue this kind of agency. These agencies will save time and money by not pursuing unmarketable product ideas.

When looking for an agency, ask many questions. Do not be shy. Everybody has the right to be inquisitive and definitely the right to know about the prospective agency. Look at their brochures and past clients. You can perform a very easy background check with the Better Business Bureau on the internet. This is a free service to the public.

Think about it. All you need to do is create a new innovative product and follow through with the paper work. Once you have file all the forms filed and paid the fees, you just have to sit back and wait. The wait for the actual patent will take about a year from the time of signing up with the agency. Meanwhile, you can still focus on your regular job and not worry about the invention.

The agency will routinely send the appropriate forms to your home and when needed, will meet with you at their office. In effect, you are paying for the patent application and its preparation. Moreover, the most important fact is that you are paying them for using their established contacts of potential buyers. This is a advantageous since it is so difficult to go door to door with a new product. Usually all companies will not listen to unknown people trying to sell their products and doing cold calls on their front door.

Once a person does have someone who wants to purchase the patent license, he would also need to pursue an international patent. This will cost approximately $30,000 but is worth the protection. So far, the description has been in the U.S. market and the potential profits you can make. There is still the international field where the product idea can bring in more profits for the inventor. The agency will convey this fact to you.

For example, the agency my partner and I are currently using cost us approximately $12,000 per product idea. Having a partner helped me reduce my cost down to $6,000 per product. Because of this relatively small fee, we were free to pursue two other ideas within weeks of each other. The amount of work we put into our product goals all equalizes in the end. This is something you must remember. This way neither one will feel overworked.

Again, you as the inventor will have to think of this venture as an investment. Even if only one product idea is licensed, the potential thousands of percent of return in our investment is worth all the effort. This should be very acceptable for any inventor.

Another example of an account follows. A friend's uncle pursued an invention and got his patent on his own. His main idea was to sell the idea to a company and went about going door to door. He even traveled out of state looking for buyers. Remember, he still has a regular job and had to pay for his own airfare and other travel expenses. This went of for months and finally ended without a single interest. My friend told me the total cost reached up to $45,000, which cannot be recovered.

There is another example where a person spent about thousands of dollars in just trying to get a patent. This does not include the manufacturing costs and marketing costs. It seemed that the patent lawyer he had hired was very expensive and took his sweet time in filing. You must know that there will be unscrupulous lawyers who will take advantage of clients. This is cost just covered the patent application. It does not cover the marketing research and other services in contacting potential buyers.

You must remember another thing that once one product idea is submitted, you must not stop. If you are feeling very creative, make more ideas and submit it when you have the appropriate funds. You and your partner should spend the majority of the time meeting, brainstorming, and finalizing the ideas.

You must get into a habit of writing down any product idea that comes to mind. Be sure to always have a pen, paper nearby at home, and work. No matter how ridiculous the idea may be, just write it down. The reason is that you can improve it later. It may also spark a very different product in a different type of use.

This is where the fifty-fifty method of sharing the profits comes in very handy, no matter who does what. It will make your lives so much easier. It frees the mind to focus on the important work of thinking of innovations. The most important thing that should be on both your minds is the money that will come from your personal work. This is the ultimate goal. Do not be obsessed of getting any old patent just to have your name on it. You will waste thousands of dollars.

Patents and Your Employer

Do not be fooled into thinking that owning a patent is such a big honor or something that is unattainable. You would be wasting your time if you just want to get your name on a patent, especially if you pursue it personally with your own money. Even if you pursue one in your workplace and the company pays for all the application fees. There is no real benefit or substantial reward from getting your name on a patent. The patent will not give you recognition in your company. Nor will you receive special treatment. All you will receive is the customary pat on the back. After a few months, the workplace is still the same and you will be treated still the same.

There are so many different patents that you will encounter during a patent search. You will find it very sad to see that many people apply for patents just to have their names on a patent. Remember that there are the application fees and lawyer fees that a person would pay which can reach thousands of dollars, depending on the patent lawyer hired. Some of the patents are very ridiculous and not even marketable. Yet, these people actually still want to get the patent.

Do not hint to your colleagues about any ideas no matter how trivial it may seem. Do not divulge your invention to anyone at work. If you want to play it safe, pursue the patent later after a change of job. Remember, the payoff could be millions of dollars and instant retirement. Would you give ten million dollars to a stranger?

Even if your background is other than an engineering field, you can still create a product idea and pursue a patent using an agency. It does not matter whether you are a doctor, dentist, mechanic, accountant, or bank clerk. You do not need a detailed background about patent laws and the engineering field. You can still create an innovative product and acquire the patent. Nothing is stopping you, other than yourself.

So, think of a product idea and pursue it with or without a business partner. Your workplace may even inspire you to develop something unique. You may find that people may need a new type of tool or new office equipment, which you can apply for a patent. You may find a new way to use a product by making a small modification to it. This may be enough to make it qualify for a possible patent.

8

Real Estate

Saving for a Home

The purchase of a house must be the number one investment goal you must have instead of paying an apartment rent. If you were to rent, the only acceptable rent would be from your parents. You do not lose the money to a stranger. You help your parents by providing them with extra cash. They usually do not require a high rent, which helps you save more money.

If you were you to pay apartment rent, you could almost never purchase the house in that time. The rental cost will drain your bank account so much and you would be hardly save any money. This is why you must rent from your parents no matter what.

You must persevere in living with your parents. They are there to support and help you in this great big step. Do not take it hard if you think they are not giving you your privacy. You can always go to a library or other place to think. Do not become frustrated if you cannot entertain a date or friends at your parent's house. All you have to tell them is that you are saving money to purchase a house. You can also take your date to a nice restaurant.

You must have a personal budget to help save money in order to buy a nice house for yourself. This simple rule applies to you and your spouse should you have one. You and your spouse need to agree on personal expenses. You both need agree on how to allocate funds to cover them.

Write on a piece of paper all the actual expenses that you incur on a daily, weekly, monthly and yearly basis. Include items such as: car insurance; car payments; car oil changes; day care center; current rent payment to your parents; baby-sitting; food and other home groceries; restaurant eating; vacations; credit card payments. Anything that has to be paid out by you (or your spouse if applicable) must be included. You must then adjust the daily, weekly and yearly expenses to a monthly figure. This will give you all the cash flow out coming from you on a monthly basis, which easier to use.

Now take your income (include your spouse's if applicable) and convert to a monthly basis. You then subtract the total monthly expenses from the total monthly income. The result will give you an idea of how much money you can save. It will also help you calculate the appropriate date when you will have cash, say $10,000 or $25,000 in your savings.

Knowing when you can have the large sum of cash is critical to your house buying. This gives you a definite target date when you can actually start looking for a house. You can already see from the cash flow list that you may still have room for reducing your expenses. You are now in effect creating a working budget that you will need to meet.

If you have a computer, you can create your budget in a spreadsheet. You can adjust the spreadsheet and make hypothetical scenarios of lowering or raising expenses. It gives you a realistic picture of your financial situation. For example, cable T.V. is a luxury item, which you do not really need. If you can live without it for now, do so.

You must be comfortable with the budget you have created. You must be happy with the amount of cash you are allocating for food, vacations and other necessities and luxury items. You can try the budget out for a few months and make any necessary adjustments. Once you are happy with the budget, you must then adhere to it. You need discipline and to take full responsibility for the budget. You must stay focus with the budget in order to achieve your goal of owning a house.

You must also create a new separate budget and spreadsheet that is tailored for the situation of you already owning a house. This budget will include the mortgage and escrow payments that you will have to make. You must also include the following items: house insurance; heating and electric bills; phone bills, water and sewage bills. This budget will show you your appropriate monthly mortgage payments you can make without stretching your savings. You will also see that it is equal to an apartment rental cost. Try to have a good amount of cash, say $10,000 minimum in your bank account after closing on the house. This ensures that you have some cash for unexpected home repairs you may have to do. It can also be used to help you furnish the house with small items aside from any donations that your family has given you.

Remember that the mortgage payment is a tax shelter for you (and your spouse). In addition, the house you buy will appreciate. You become better prepared and fully conscious of your cash flows when you do these budgets.

While you are saving money according to your budget, you need to maintain a good credit record. Always pay your credit card bills, car payments, and any other bills in your name on time. Never spend more money than you can afford. Buy things with your credit card, which you can pay all of it the next billing period. This way you are not wasting money with the high interest cost on your credit card.

Save all your work pay stubs of two years and W-2 Forms. You will need these documents for the bank when you apply for your mortgage loan. Doing these things will make the loan application easier.

Looking for a House

When you have enough cash in your bank account, you can start looking for a house. Drive around the neighborhood you want to live. If you have a child or children, look for a house very close to either the elementary school or high school. If you are lucky and get a house close to school, your children can walk to school. You will have the peace of mind that they are close to home. In addition, being close to a school makes the house appreciate faster.

Look for a house where you will have a minimum amount of home remodeling. Look very closely at the ceiling and window areas to make sure that there are no water leaks. Discoloration in the ceilings and walls are sure signs of water leaks from rain or broken water pipes. Try to find an all brick house rather than one with siding. The brick house can withstand the wind and feels safer during a storm. The siding type will move and make noises against the house.

Never buy a house on a busy street, especially if you have a child. There are too many cars and trucks going fast. The drivers can easily hit your child. No house is worth this type of trouble. Try to buy a house with two or more bedrooms, but that is within your budget. This also holds true for two or more bathrooms. The reason is that they are good selling points when you decide to sell the house.

A garage is another feature that is good to have. Depending on your budget, a bigger garage is always better to have. It helps make the house appreciate more and you can use it for more storage space.

Do not forget the old adage of location, location, location. Houses will appreciate very fast in the following conditions: in the city near the downtown area or business districts; near a university and other schools; near the lake front; near affluent neighborhoods. Some of these may be too high priced for your budget, but you can search still look at the neighboring area every other week.

It is acceptable to sign up with a realtor to help you find a house. Find one that you are comfortable with whom you can work. Ask around your family first if they know somebody. A family member may know one and even a real estate lawyer. Use them because they will treat you well, since they know you are a relative with one of their past clients.

Purchased House

Once you have bought the house, do not spend a lot of money right away in furnishing it. Settle down first in the house and try to use any extra furniture and kitchen equipment that your family can donate. Ask around for sofas and tables also. There is no shame in doing this. Remember that you are just starting to live as a homeowner. There will be other expenses and possible minor repairs that you may need to do. Live in the house for about a year to see how it stands throughout the four seasons.

You will be able to learn that small things may need to be repaired such as the water faucet. You may even learn that you may need a new water heater, which has an average cost of $500 depending on the size of the unit. Other items that you may have to repair are the sewage system; air conditioning and heater; refrigerator, oven, dishwasher and kitchen vent; toilets and bathroom sinks and lighting fixtures. These are just a few items usually come up in owning a house.

You may want to paint the house immediately before moving all the furniture into it. If there is hardwood floor and it needs refinishing, this should be done before moving into the house. You would not have to sleep through the dust and paint fumes. Once everything is finished, you are essentially moving into a clean house. Be proud of what you have accomplished within a short time.

When you have purchased your first house, stay there for a few years and always try to maintain its appearance and structure. You must do some work every year or have something done by a professional. You must keep your lawn looking good by fertilizing and using crab grass control at the start of spring. You can buy these from any home improvement stores and easily broadcast it on your lawn.

In the middle of summer around June, use grub control on your lawn. This will help keep the grass looking green and healthy. The grubs will feed off the root system you do not take care of them. Cut the grass by yourself every week to keep it healthy. You can use a manual lawn mower, which is very easy and safe to use. If you have to get a powered lawn mower, get an electric one. The gas-powered types are a bit more dangerous and you have all the fumes blowing in your face. These fumes are not good for your lungs.

You can add fertilizer again in August to help revitalize the yard. Finally, you need to aerate the ground around September. You can buy a simple aeration tool for about $25 and do it yourself. Discipline yourself to do these yard work, which help you save more money. Hiring someone to work on your lawn will average about $100 per month. This $100 more that you can put into your bank account.

Of course, throughout the spring, summer and fall seasons you need to keep everything looking clean in both your front and backyard. Rake the leaves and small branches that may have fallen on your yard. Always throw out all the lawn debris. Clean all the gutters of leaves and branches in the gutters on both the house and garage. These will clog up your gutter during a rainstorm. The water can then do damage to your house and garage.

Do not let the leaves stay on your lawn. This will rot the grass underneath and create a swampy feel in your yard. All the work you had done during the summer would have been for nothing.

You must also do some landscaping or vegetable planting during the summer. This helps you connect with nature and the surroundings. You feel better after doing a good hour or two of yard work. In the fall, you can harvest anything you may have planted. Some typical vegetables that are great to plant are tomatoes, peppers, eggplant, and green onions. These are easy to take grow and very good for cooking.

There are projects where you will have to hire professionals. Whenever you have to hire someone, you can also look in the phone book for someone. Some of the people you would need are contractors, plumbers, electricians and maintenance engineers. For example, you will need to have your sewer drain cleaned out every other year, depending on your drain usage. You must do this so that your drain does not back up into your house.

You will need to tuck point the bricks and replace the roof when it becomes necessary. Again, you can find someone in the phone book. You do not want any water intrusion going through the walls and ceiling during a rainstorm. Always check the walls and ceiling during a storm to make sure there is no leak. Maintain your water heater, air conditioner and heater at every year. All these things contribute to the appreciation of your home.

Home Remodeling

Remodeling your house is another smart investment that you do. However, do this after living about one or two years in the house. This helps you build up more cash savings while you discover other things in the house that you may want to renovate. You should remodel a house where you know that you will live there for a long time. You would not want to remodel a home and then sell it after year or two. The reason is that you would hardly recapture the cost you put into the remodeling. In addition, you would not be able to enjoy the hard work you put into your home.

Watch your local public T.V. shows that demonstrate home remodeling projects. These shows are free and full of very valuable information. One episode may show you how to repair and finish your hardwood floor. Another show may demonstrate how to replace a washer in your kitchen faucet. There could be a series of episodes where they remodel the whole house. You will learn many tips and ideas of what can be done to any rooms in the house. You can also estimate the costs for each phase of your home remodeling.

However, you must do your homework first before committing to the renovation. Look around the lumberyard and home remodeling stores. Write down the costs of the things you will have to buy. Include everything from a paintbrush to a new oven, if you need it. Shop around in different stores to find the best prices and sales. If a store offers a year of zero percent financing by using their credit card, do it. Defer as much payments you can and always go for the bargains. Try not to buy the most expensive items. You can live on the medium end items and it would still look nice.

Take notes and pictures of sample rooms in any home building stores. You can always find other places where a similar item is offered at a lower price. For example, I used several stores for different items and equipments in my kitchen-remodeling project. I bought the cabinets and appliances from different stores. It just so happened that the store offered the zero percent financing for one and a half year by using their store brand credit card. I took the opportunity and saved hundreds of dollars.

The highest cost in any home projects can actually be the labor costs. The material costs and appliances will vary depending on your taste and budget. Keep your budget in mind at all times. You will also find that as you remodel, surprises usually happen as the project progresses. There could be hidden problems in the room or kitchen you are remodeling. For example, the wall I wanted to knock down dividing the dining room and kitchen had three air ducts inside them.

These had to be rerouted to the kitchen wall and over the ceiling back to their original junction. There were also electrical wirings in the wall that had to be rerouted.

Make drawings of your remodeling ideas first on paper. Sketch the ideas thoroughly and include all the cabinets, light fixtures, and appliances. If you want to knock down walls, include this in the sketch. Once you have a first draft, leave it alone for a day or two. You may decide to change it around and add other things. Include all the wish list that you would want to accomplish in the renovation. It is better to try to include the total extent of the wish lists because then you would not have to endure another renovation where your house will be in disarray. You would have the inconvenience one time only.

However, do the extra renovation ideas only if it is within your budget. If the costs are running too high, then look back at your renovation ideas. Maybe you can exclude high luxury items such as a new refrigerator or garbage disposal. These items can be included later and do not require major work in the house.

Depending on the complexity of the remodeling, you can probably do some or all the remodeling by yourself. However, do this only if you are good at doing construction work. Also, think of how much time you can actually allocate for the project. If you can tolerate having a messy home for some length of time, then go ahead and do the work.

Otherwise, you can look through the local phone book for home improvement contractors. Get at least three quotes and pick the best one you like. Make sure that you have a list of work that you want them to do. You must do this in order to avoid any over charges to you. This also protects you from the contractors not doing a specific task. Always ask for how long the contractors will take to finish the job.

The contractors can buy the materials for you. This is good especially for the large pieces of plywood or drywall that you may need. They can haul it and use their own truck to bring it to your place. Make sure that they will also clean up the debris and haul it away. You must tell them that you do not want to throw out the debris in your regular garbage collection. Depending on the amount of work, the garbage generated can be very large.

If friends or family has recommended the contractors, then try them. You can probably leave them the house key so that they can work on your house everyday. This will definitely expedite the home remodeling.

Depending on what you are remodeling, you will not be able to use that room for some time. Keep this in mind and have patience. Sometimes there are things that you cannot rush.

Never hire a relative to remodel anything in your home. Some relatives are trustworthy and others may take advantage of you. You will never know until you have hired them.

You may be tempted to hire a person because of the very low price. There are some drawbacks to doing this. Their standard procedure is to keep getting jobs and lining it up sequentially. The problem with this is that they will spread out all the work over months. Where your house would have taken probably three weeks to finish, now would take up to six months.

These types of contractors have no loyalty to anybody. No matter how much you call and complain, they will not finish your house per your request. They do this because they have already locked you in with their pricing. They always want to pick up new clients and keep squeezing small miscellaneous jobs in front of your house. They do this because they are picking up all the money that they can. They think they are the king of the world and that they owe you nothing.

In reality, these people have much to learn about providing customer service. Yes, it would be great to find a contractor that will provide the highest customer service. The problem is that some contractors just do not want to give that service. They are content in getting any jobs that come their way.

Once you complete the remodeling, you can enjoy your house again. However, make sure you inspect everything to make sure there are no problems. For example, you must make sure there are no gas leaks if you purchase a new gas oven. You must repeatedly check for leaks the following weeks because it may take time to surface.

Live very simply and decorate your house sparingly. Use minimal furniture and only ones that you really need. Do not buy anything extra. You will just create clutter in your house. You may not even need end tables and lamps to put on them. Sometimes a single floor lamp is better for the look and lighting. It also helps free up space in the house making it look bigger.

The best things you can use for the windows are inexpensive curtains. However, this will really depend on your taste. Do not indulge with too many small knick-knacks and other cheap items that you might eventually throw out. You are just wasting your money in doing this. Always purchase items that will help make your life easier. You do not have to buy the most expensive items.

9

Vacation Travels

Destinations

You will need a vacation especially once you have joined the American work force. Your vacation time should be an enjoyable experience whether you are staying at home, going out of state or traveling out of the country. There are so many places to visit. You should prioritize where you would like to go first.

You will find many factors to consider in planning your vacation destination place. The main ones that can be considered are available time off from work or school; the vacation cost falling within your budget; whether you need a travel companion or not and if your destination is seasonal.

If you are still in college, you should just take about a week off following your finals. You can take a vacation possibly within two to three hours from your home. The reason you should not go any farther is that you are still young and do not really know how to fend for yourself. You will have other opportunities for a more extensive vacation once you start working full time.

You may not even have a major credit card yet which is typically a good thing to carry. You can use the credit card in cases of emergencies whenever you are traveling. Besides the safety consideration, you have no extra cash for a vacation that will require hotels, airfare, and entertainment.

Now, if you already have graduated from college and have a steady job, then you can plan a more interesting and fun vacation. You can travel to great cities in other countries such as the Philippines, Puerto Rico, Mexico, Spain, and Greece. You will learn to appreciate your history classes in high school as you see first hand the various landmarks and other historical sites.

Going on a vacation with a friend is a good idea because you can share the hotel lodging costs. The hotel costs can range from $70 to $200 a night per person. This will of course depend whether you are going to a very popular city and especially during the peak seasons. Actually, some places can be worth the costs during the busy seasons such as the Greek Islands Mykonos and Hydra. The main beaches are open and can be enjoyed by everyone during the summer in July. This is of course the best time to sit in the cafes dotting the islands. The restaurants are at their best at this time when all the seafood is available.

You could go to the Greek Islands during the off-season but you will have limited fun. There will not be many activities for you to do other than walk around the city. Many of the bars and nightclubs may not even be open.

Be sure to check the newspapers and the internet for vacation packages offered by travel agencies. These offers do really work and will give you affordable packages. There are packages to countries such as Greece, Spain, Mexico, Jamaica, and Italy. There are packages that offer all-inclusive pricing. For example, you can go to popular Mexican destinations such as Cancun for a week. This could cost you $700 U.S. dollars per person. Even though the package has to be purchased for two people, this is great bargain. The price includes your air fare, hotel lodging, and food. You will not have to pay anymore cash other than extra entertainment. You will find vacation packages that include your drinks.

Other than the internet, ask around your circle of friends and colleagues. They will definitely let you know their vacation experiences and whether they have enjoyed the places, they visited. Everyone is different. People look for different experiences in any vacation. Some people may just want to sit in café, eat the regional cuisine, or do a lot of sightseeing. Others may want a more active nightlife and go bar hopping. The point is that you must plan your vacation on what you would like to experience more.

When you do have an idea of what type of vacation you want to see, then you can plan your vacation accordingly. This will help you better find the right travel companion who shares your vacation plan. You should go ahead and buy the travel books sold in the bookstores. These books do contain useful information about the city you are planning to visit. There are so many tips about how to get around the city and what to see. It also lists where the best restaurants or local diners are located. You can then start to enjoy your vacation as you tailor your itinerary. Make sure you make a list of things you want to do and sites to see.

Besides the books, you can call the established tourism board located in major U.S. cities for any country you want to visit. These agencies will send you any brochures, maps, and books at no cost at all. For example, call information and ask for the tourism phone number for Italy. You can request from the Italian agency to send you information about the city you will be visiting. They will also be able to tell you about activities and festivals that will be happening on the days you will be there.

When you do travel to a foreign country, it is a good idea to take a translation book or electronic translator. This will help you get around much more easily and possibly help you get out of trouble. If you have time, try to learn some key phrases. Do not break any laws in the country you are visiting. Definitely read about any simple local laws from a travel book. Also, bring a copy of your passport and two passport size photos. This will help expedite you getting a new passport should you lose your current one while vacationing.

Packing for Travel

You must always travel light. Hauling a big luggage is very uncomfortable. The best thing you can do is to take one medium carry-on luggage. You should get one with wheels if you are planning to move about many times. Otherwise, a backpack or shoulder type bag will do just great. These are very easy to carry and move around.

If you have a large luggage, it will have to be checked-in. Two bad things can happen to your luggage. People can easily steal things inside your luggage. You will not know until you are already at your hotel. The other is that the luggage may be missing. The handlers could mistakenly put your luggage on another flight. If you really have to check-in a large luggage, try to have a picture of it. This will help the airport authorities track it down should it be lost.

You must bring only small amounts of essential things. This will help make your bag light to carry. Take a small tube of toothpaste with you. Carry enough socks and underwear to last a few days. You can wash these when they need to be cleaned. Take a pair of jeans and undergarments you think you will need. If your clothes can go with a pair of nice leisure shoes, just take that one pair. If you do not really need a hair dryer, leave it behind.

Many of the hotels do have stores where you can buy common toiletries just like in the U.S. Some also provide hair dryers in the rooms anyway. You may be surprised that you may not even need the hair dryer as you begin to relax more. You will find that you look just fine without all the hassles of fixing your hair.

You must bring a camera to take pictures of the places you are visiting. The pictures will give you good memories of your vacations. Bring enough rolls of film for your vacation. You could probably get away with two 24 exposures. When you are back at home, wait for specials and coupons to develop the film.

However, the best camera to bring these days will be a digital camera. You do not have to use any more film. You will just need to store the images on the memory chip. You can also delete any unwanted images immediately. You can send the images by email to your friends and family.

When you are traveling in the states or overseas, do not bring anything that is very valuable. Do not bring your most expensive watch, sunglasses or other jewelries. You could easily forget these items or leave them in the hotel drawers. There will be people who will find these and steal them. This is one of the inconveniences of traveling anywhere.

If you do bring valuables, then carry them at all times whenever you leave the hotel room. Place them on the nightstand closest to your bed. This will help you remember to put on your expensive jewelries every morning. Always carry your cash and traveler's checks with all the time. Do not leave these items behind because hotel workers can easily steal them.

Protecting Yourself and Your Valuables

Be very careful in tourist areas where there are groups of people watching performers or exhibitions. These are great target places for thieves and pickpockets. While you are watching the performers, the pickpockets will lift off your wallet from your pants. This also goes for women's purses being picked. The way they work is very organized. Sometimes the performers are part of the gang who circles the crowd looking for easy preys. They will use full teamwork in order to get as much cash and credit cards.

There are also very aggressive thieves. They will snatch a purse from a woman and run off somewhere. A team member may even offer his services to you and take off after the thief. This way you lower your guard and not raise any more attention.

You must remember that every city have poor people living there. Some will resort to thievery in order to buy food and clothing. Unfortunately, others may use the money for buying alcohol or drugs.

In poor countries, which many people are now visiting, the level of danger can be much higher. There will be organized gangs who commit crimes that are more serious. There are places where a band will actually kidnap people for ransom money. These abductions will be more frequent with tourists going into the countryside or forests. This is another example of why you should not wear very expensive items. You could be marked as a wealthy person with family members ready to pay a large sum of money for your release.

Another bad situation that can happen is if an unscrupulous person hands you what appears to be an innocent looking package. Under no circumstance should you accept the package. Even if it were opened in front of your eyes and the contents exposed.

These people are very clever and could still have narcotics hidden in the container. You will be tried and convicted according to that country's legal system. If all the evidence points to you and they cannot locate the person, you will be the one to go to jail. Do not take any boxes from strangers or just recent acquaintances back to the U.S. They can put illegal things in them. Think about it. These people should just be able to ship these boxes.

You must inspect your luggage thoroughly in your hotel room when you are packing to leave. Empty everything out on the bed and repack it meticulously. This way you will be sure that you do not leave anything behind. You also get the peace of mind that you did not pack anything that is unfamiliar to you. This is to make sure that no one got into your room and put anything into your luggage such as drugs.

You must always know the contents of your luggage. Never leave it out of your sight. Never have someone watch over it while you go to the toilet or buy a cup of coffee. There can be people who will quickly insert boxes of illegal drugs into your luggage. They are using you as a courier so that their merchandise is delivered to the U.S. The bad thing is that you will be the one to go to jail.

When you are planning your vacation, stay away from troubled regions. Do not go near these countries because you will be endangering your life. You will not find these areas to be fun and you will be wasting your vacation time and money. You are better off going to safe cities where you can relax.

If traveling on your own or with friends does not appeal to you at all, you can sign up with a tour group. Many tours are structured to visit different cities sequentially. The great thing about this is that the tour cost includes the airfare, hotel lodging, some food, and the transportation to take you to each city destination. They will also take care of all the visas you will need when the tour crosses an international border.

The hotels you will stay in are all modern and quite comfortable. You will have to share the room with someone else so it may be a good idea to travel with a friend. At other hotels, you may actually have to share the hotel room with four people. This is one of the disadvantages of traveling with a tour group.

The travel agency creates itineraries to take you to the popular tourist areas and even off beaten paths. The tour's main goal is to give you a memorable time in visiting the places. The tour guide can give you many recommendations on where to go on your own if you wish to go about the city. This will be good to do in cities that are relatively calm and safe. If you do go walking alone, do not stay out too late especially at night. Many cities also have curfews that are strictly enforced.

Be aware also that some of the public transportations such as the trains and taxis have operating time limits. They will not be available very late in the evening. The main thing you can do is to venture close to your hotel within walking distance. Also, ask your hotel concierge if they close the doors late at night. You actually could possibly become locked out of your hotel.

In the tour group, a dedicated tour guide will walk you through all the steps and procedures in the tour. The guide will give historical information on the sites and any interesting stories. The tour agency will also provide all the tickets for any events that the tour advertise for you to see. This includes extra transportation such as ferry rides and cable car rides.

An organized tour provides a sense of peace and safety. The tour guide will have the necessary resources should anything happen. The agency will be able to provide help immediately.

The tour will take you to all sorts of stores and other souvenir shops. There will be plenty of time for shopping and milling around. Be sure to spend your money wisely and not buy anything that will be too large to carry back onto the airplane. Never buy anything that looks even remotely cheap. It will most likely break up and you would have wasted your money. You will be better off spending your money on good food or something that you can really appreciate.

Unless you know how to operate a motorcycle, do not rent one or even a moped. These can be very dangerous and you will be putting yourself in harms way. If you read the brochures, some even give warnings on renting these modes of transportation. There are cases where tourists have lost their lives riding these machines and have them go out of control.

When you do go on a vacation, you must secure your house so that nobody breaks into it. You must buy a lamp timer so that your house will have light in the evening hours, which will give the illusion that someone is still living there. You must also call the U.S Post Office to hold your mail from the start of your vacation and up to your return. This way your mailbox will not be overflowing with mail. You must leave a copy of you itinerary with a family member or a friend. People will then be able to get in touch with you in case of emergencies.

10

Friends

Learning about Friends

From childhood all the way through adulthood, you will have friends in your life. The true friends will be there to encourage you in your endeavors. They will give you proper support in your projects when you need it. Friends will be glad to help paint your house or even help remodel a room in your house. Friends will be there to provide cheers whether you need it or not. These true friends will look out for anyone in any situations that arises. They will provide honest compliments in your life.

Be advised that not all people are true friends. It is necessary for you to learn how to determine which people can really be true friends. It is very important to be aware of people. This involves knowing what their true intentions are towards you. You must observe and watch their body language as this is a good indication on their intentions.

Specifically, you must watch how people smile. A person's smile can actually be a signal if he or she is telling the truth. Many people actually give a fake smile to particular responses. These are forced smiles where the ends of the mouth are forced up. A true smile comes from a complete facial expression. It ranges from the eyebrows, to the eyes, to the cheeks and all the way to the lips. Be very aware of this facial expression. You will be able to tell the difference between a true person and a self-centered individual.

The people with the fake smiles have something to hide; or just do not really know the correct answer to a question; or the course of action to take. They think that they are always right and that you are wrong. Their motives are set on their gaining something from you and their other friends. Fake smiles will shine through any person who is not sincere. An honest smile involves your whole face and at times even your body. Learn how to read the signs from strangers and people just have met. You must be careful of uncaring people that you might think are friends.

These people may actually have low opinions of everyone. They could think that other people are very naïve or just plain stupid. Some will tolerate their presence because of common acquaintances. These uncaring people may actually use their friends just to get on higher ground. These people will never look out for anyone. They do not have anyone's best interest in mind.

They could use you by borrowing things from you. You must be careful of people who always need something. They could be borrowing a camera or set of luggage but that could be the extent of it. They tend to use you as their source of "assets". Notice that they will even neglect to return the things they have borrowed from you. If something has been broken, they will tell you a story and try to get out of replacing the things.

In restaurants, make sure you divide the bills properly. Do not back down and give more money than your uncaring friends. They will notice this and take advantage of you. There will be many times when you go out socially with friends. Keep a mental tab on what you have ordered and how much you should be paying. This is just to make sure these people do not use you as their bank account.

Demeaning Friends

You must be very selective of people you see on a daily basis. Listen to how they talk to colleagues and other people they have just met. You can make great comparisons on how they treat friends and strangers. Be particularly attentive in their conversion. You must listen for racial jokes. Do not contribute to their racial jokes but just smile briefly and walk away. Other people could be watching and they will associate you with these bad people. Do not indulge in these jokes or condone their actions. They are demeaning and no one in the world would really like their ethnic background slandered.

The person who likes to tell racial jokes will also speak out racial slurs in time. The person will often do it in front of his own kind who eventually will add to the indignant behavior. It is their human nature to keep telling demeaning jokes. It is a bad habit they have developed and has become second nature to them. They get bolder especially with their own kind supporting them. They will soon think they are above everyone else, even the friends that have supported them before.

The sad thing is that this type of person will eventually give out insults. They will find instances and events, which they will use to justify their prejudice. Deep down they harbor ill feelings about other ethnic groups. Eventually, these people will resort to giving out racial slurs. You must break away from these people as soon as you hear any type of slander. They are not to be trusted and do not deserve your friendship.

Some people after time will treat you rudely. They will disguise their disrespect of calling you names and labels as jokes. They will start making fun of you. They will even say that you are uptight and should loosen up, just because you expressed your feeling that you do not wish slander. These people actually have personal problems themselves. They could just be showing their true colors after all these times. When people become comfortable with friends, they will make a mistake and say what they really feel. Remember this moment when it appears because this is the time you will know they are not your true friends.

These disrespectful people will create situations where they can talk down on ethnic people. Unfortunately, other ethnic people may never hear it. They will even use opportunities to point out so-called stereotypes on people. There will be cover-ups by their other prejudiced friends who will try to help this bad person. It is very important that you find out which people can be your friend and which ones are prejudiced.

Learning how to read people is very important particularly when meeting colleagues at a new workplace. It is a necessity for you to know who can be trusted in an office environment. Many potential people can become friends. You must be sure who will be a true friend. A good honest friend at the office will help encourage colleagues. They will give good honest advice when needed most and possibly even help people advance in their career.

At times, it becomes necessary to break away from some friends. The main reason for doing this can range from disrespect to flat out insolence. They could be harassing you constantly and periodically. Stop seeing them and stop communicating with them. There is no need to keep the company of people who have no regard for other people. If someone is always making you angry, drop this friend. You can always find new and better friends. Do not be afraid or feel any remorse from breaking away from these untrue friends. Your life will become easier and your stress will be relieved.

If a friend is too sociable with your girlfriend or boyfriend, drop this friend. Do not take your date to any social events such as dancing and dinner with this intruding friend. This person will take opportunities to get close to our date.

There is no reason for anyone to be too friendly to your date. People do this because their motivation is to get another person's girlfriend/boyfriend.

Stop attending parties they may host. If somebody else is holding the party, go ahead and attend the party. You do not have to talk much with this type of friend. Exchange salutations normally and do it in a professional manner. That should be the end of it. Give a solid excuse and talk to someone else. Walk away from them. Do not volunteer any information because these people will use it. Do not show the true intent as this would cause them to start a confrontation in front of people.

Stop initiating phone calls or even emails to these untrue friends. They probably will not even try very hard in calling. This is when their actual motives may even show. You should also stop lending things to these people before breaking off. They will never return your things. You must not do any favors for them. This opens up situations where they will take advantage of it.

Pay attention to advices they give you. If you know or think that some of the advices are bad, then that friend does not care about you. He is trying to lead you astray. This is most dangerous especially if you are misled in your workplace. That friend may even want something harmful to happen to you.

Many people do not know this, but untrue friends actually contribute to stress. They tend to stunt the development of good people. Many discouraging words come from them and the majority of it being false. They will even spread rumors and lies about you that other people eventually hear. This kind of talk is very annoying to anyone. Do not give any excuses for rumors to spread because it will multiply.

Rumors happen because of jealousy by these types of friends. The reason could be a good sense of humor they see in somebody else or they feel inferior to another person's success and abilities. They have no real affinity in being good friends. Remember they lack proper family values. They have not been educated properly and do not know the meaning of friendship.

You must believe in your own abilities and convictions. There should be no doubt that you will always do the right thing. If rumors should come across your path, you must ignore it or even counter it.

Good Friends

You must look for other people properly trained in good family values. These are the friends that must be kept when found. These true friends give encouragement to family members and friends that they make. With luck, a good friend to find is one that will actually complement your personality. Separately, both of you will get through school without much trouble. Should you team together, you could inconceivably be very successful in school, work and life. Should you even decide to work together on personal projects, you two could form your own company.

Your lifestyle will actually become more relaxed and enjoyable with good friends around you. You would not have to worry about rumors or verbal abuses that usually come from bad friends. A true friend would not take advantage of you and he would not take you for granted. You would not have to watch how you and your friend act in social events because of what an untrue friend might say or do. You would really have to be careful of the company you keep. It is true that many observers will judge people from the friends or people with whom they always socialize.

You and a true friend would not experience inconvenience anymore from untrue friends who do not keep appointments. This is nothing new. Many people have been through this type of frustration. For example, it is never a good feeling to wait for someone who is late on purpose. Let it go and concentrate more on other personal business. Go and spend more time with true friends rather than fretting over an uncaring one.

Your trustworthy friend is a great travel companion for vacations. You would have total agreement in planning which city and sights you two would want to visit. The vacation would truly be relaxing for both of you. No one wants to travel and spend the vacation staying inside a hotel room because of an uncooperative travel companion.

The expenses would also be well budgeted in the choices of the hotels and restaurants. You both know you could trust each other for any emergencies. This is so important because should something unpleasant happen while overseas, a true friend can really help and provide comfort. For example, someone may catch a fever or get into an accident. Your true friend will help ease your discomfort and find the proper care for you.

There would be camaraderie between true friends and this helps in the total relaxation you seek in a good vacation. There are so many sights and things to do on vacations. You must enjoy your life and should not have to worry about making someone your friend.

Friendship develops through respect of each other. You must be honest with the friend and always do the right things. These are some points that you must remember regarding the Asian way of having friends. It goes along the way of respecting your elders. Do not lie or steal from anyone and your friends.

These points also apply to your boyfriend or girlfriend. Be honest to them and treat them with respect, as you would want to be treated. Do not cheat on your girlfriend or boyfriend. Pay attention and listen to what your girlfriend or boyfriend is saying. You must always keep these points in mind at all times.

If you see your friend drinking too much and then driving, stop them. Tell them they have a drinking problem and must stop it. If you see your friends smoking or starting to take drugs, help them stop. Should a friend go through some family problems or tragic events, be there for your friend and help them. Listen to them and give your best honest advice. Sometimes your friend will have an emotional problem, which could be too great for you to handle alone. You must advice your friend to see a professional doctor. Be a credit to your heritage and show how Asians have fortitude.

Defending Asians

Never, ever make fun of other Asians. Never be rude to other Asians in particular. Never, ever make stereotypical comments about Asians and other ethnic groups of people. Do not propagate any comments that contribute to stereotypes of people. Even if your friend starts an ethnic joke or joins in one, do not join the friend. This is not good behavior to follow. Be your own person with your own mind. Do the right thing and the right action. Stop the ethnic joke.

You must defend other Asians whenever you can. You can do this in conversations, social events and especially at work. It is very important that you speak up and try to dissuade any bad remarks or rumors that may surround an Asian person you know. Even if the person is not there, you must defend him or her and find out why people are talking badly about that person. Correct people immediately when they make bad comments and stereotypical comments. Tell the Asian person you are defending what the other people were saying. You must be honest with this person and try to help him deal with the indignation. There is no need to fight but help prepare him professionally.

If the bad rumors are happening at work and depending on the severity of the situation, maybe suggest to the victim to visit the corporate Human Resource. Tell the person which people are starting the rumors and to stay away from them. You must also remind the victimized person that there is no need to start rumors also against the antagonists. Both of you should just walk away from those people. Remember that you must pick your battles wisely.

All the companies that you work for will eventually have rumors spread around. Unfortunately, you will be the target one day. This is the reason why you must never tell anybody all your problems at work. Never confide to your colleagues and people that you are not very familiar. They will take things out of context and hence the rumors will start.

You must give proper advice to other Asians that need help. If you see someone poorly dressed, then tell the person to try a new makeover. Tell the person to get a new haircut and new clothes to match. If you see someone harassed by other people, go and help that person. Take the person under your wing for some time until you see some improvements. This will not take too much of your time and will be very rewarding in helping other people.

You must pass on whatever you have learned to your true Asian friends. You should always be giving help freely especially to those who are not as fortunate. Always help the underdog. This is very basic in being a good Asian with true family values

When you help other people, they can return the favor. If they ask whether you need something in return, tell them to do the same to other people. They will remember what you as an Asian have done for them. They will remember that Asians are helpful and do not expect anything in return. Your good deed will spread out like rings of waves in pool of water.

11

Stereotype

Background

There are people out there who still like to stereotype people. They label Asians as poor dressers, bad drivers and lacking in certain social skills. They make fun of the narrow eyes and the accent. Stereotyping people because of their ethnic background is not good behavior. As you would not like to be stereotyped, you should never label anybody else. Although stereotyping will continue, there are ways to change certain preconceived stereotypical notions about being Asians.

Stereotypical Behaviors

You may not be aware that you are exhibiting stereotypical behaviors in everyday life. You may be looking down at the ground while walking. You may be wearing gym shoes and old clothes at college and work. You may be speaking too softly when questioned at work. You may be speaking with a heavy accent or using improper grammar usage. You could be wearing thick plastic framed glasses and smiling too much. All these behaviors have become second nature to you through repetition.

You must learn to recognize these behaviors and traits. You need to know which behaviors you are exhibiting that is considered as stereotype. You can then stop these behaviors, which cause people to think lowly of Asians. Never give people any excuses to make fun of you and attach stereotypical connotations. Show them that you are a strong Asian and that they cannot touch you.

You can watch movies, or better yet, foreign Asian movies that have a contemporary storyline. There are even public channels now with Asian shows that you can watch. These shows have Asians in regular looking clothes ranging from leisure to business suits. They all look sharp in the clothes with nice hairstyles. You can see how they act in situations that you also experience.

You should watch martial arts movies with great masters such as Bruce Lee or Jet Li. Make them your heroes and model yourself with their behaviors. It gives you a chance to see someone that you can relate to and learn non-stereotypical behaviors. So take notes, study their behaviors, and try to mimic them.

Do not watch any shows or movies that promote stereotypes for Asians and other ethnic groups. The people who made these bad movies may be thinking it is humorous to depict other ethnic people in a stereotypical setting. Why would you want to give your hard-earned money to people who have no respect for other ethnic groups? They are all wrong. Stop and think.

The same people who perpetuate stereotypes in movies will protest also if they are the ones depicted in a derogatory manner. If you do come across one of these bad shows, tell other people not to watch them. You must alert them about these demeaning movies. You must educate them not to endorse and propagate any demeaning Asian movies.

Clothing Ideas for Men and Women

Clothes are the first things that people see on you and make their initial judgment. Do not wear old drab looking clothes. You must learn how to pick nice clothes for both your workplace and weekend attire. You can learn by observing people around you. Look at how bank tellers, hotel concierges, and even newscasters dress for their workplace. Both men and women are pleasant to view regardless of their nationalities. They also had to learn how to pick their clothes at some point in their lives. Usually the best things to do are walk around clothing stores and look at fashion magazines.

You could subscribe to various fashion type magazines. These magazines contain information on how to wear clothes and what accessories go with them. The magazines have numerous photographs and articles that go along with them. It will describe what is appropriate to wear for work and other social occasions. The magazines also show new styles of clothes that are available in the stores. If you are not sure yet whether you want to subscribe, just buy one first and see how you like it.

One thing you should know is that you do not have to purchase the exact items advertised in the magazines. Getting the exact advertised designer outfit can be very expensive. These advertisements target people who can afford to buy them and who love to wear the newest styles. You do not have to buy the very expensive items shown on the pages. You must always keep cost in mind when you are shopping for clothes. You do not want to incur too much credit card bills, which you may not be able to pay.

Just study the look, the color, and ways to accessorize the clothes from the magazines. Once you see something in the magazine that you like, check the department stores in any mall for ideas. You should go to different stores for items that match the ones you like in the magazines. This is a very good way to build up your wardrobe. You must be selective and make sure that you will be comfortable wearing the clothes you have chosen.

You must have an open mind to other things you may never have thought would look good on you. The reason is that the clothes may actually look good on you even though you still adhere to your own basic fashion ideas. For example, you may not feel comfortable with a cotton and synthetic blend shirt. However, it may look good on you as a semi-formal wear for the evening.

Work Attire for Men

For the office environment, wear leather shoes although some synthetics that look like business shoes are acceptable. In other work environment, wear the appropriate shoes that are comfortable and safe for your. Never wear athletic shoes and others that are too leisurely looking. You must always present yourself in a respectable manner whenever you are outside your home.

You can also get ideas when you watch morning shows on T.V. that will have a segment on clothes. These occasionally happen at the start of a season where the show is helping the audience with fashion tips. Some talk shows will also have segments on fashion. They like to keep the audience informed on what is in fashion.

You can also go to department stores and inquire about any upcoming fashion shows. You can get a schedule from the store manager. These shows are usually open to the public, which will not cost you anything. These shows promote their current designers, depending on the store. Make sure you go to the fashion shows where you do like their line of clothes.

Do not buy suits from stores that cater to large size people. These off the rack suits will never fit you properly. The clothes will just look terrible even after you have altered them. No amount of tailoring will make the clothes look good on you. The salesperson will obviously say the suit looks good on you because the store wants you to buy the clothes.

You can actually buy suits in specialty stores that cater to young men. Most of these stores have recently added the formal wear in their line. You will find that the clothes in these stores fit you very well and look very nice on you. They are not baggy and the materials used are comfortable. In addition, these clothes are very affordable. These stores provide a good look for you since most of their clothes coordinate with each other. You can almost buy your entire wardrobe in one place. However, you should not do this because you must have variety in your wardrobe. You can do this by shopping in different stores.

You can purchase suits with colors such as dark blue, black, and charcoal gray. Sometimes, even a light gray suit for the summer will look good on you. These are great colors to wear and match with the types of shirts mentioned above. These suits can also have stripes and the shirts will still match nicely.

You can also use the same shirt colors mentioned above with stripes. However, wear these shirts only with plain colored suits as mentioned above. Matching ties are still very easy to do with both plain and striped suits. Ties can also be the one article you can let your own personal tastes come out. Go to any store and pick a tie that immediately grabs your attention.

Do not wear shirt colors such as green, pink, red, orange, and brown. These shirts will not look very well on you whether for formal or leisurewear. These colors are especially hard to match with ties.

Casual Attire for Men

You can wear a nice black t-shirt with the suit. Never wear a shirt buttoned all the way up if you are not going to wear a tie. Always leave the top two unbuttoned. This looks much better on you. It is acceptable to loosen the tie and the shirt unbuttoned at the top for the casual look.

Do not wear plaid shirts whether they have long or short sleeves. Do not think that a plaid shirt is okay to wear even for leisure. Stay with plain colored shirts. Use colors such as black, white, light blue, tan and navy blue. These plain shirts will always go with black, dark gray and navy blue suits.

During the summer, you would want to wear lighter colored clothes and thin shirts for comfort. Cotton is especially good for this because it breathes much easier and can keep you cooler at work. What also helps is to wear loose fitting shirts.

If you have to keep wearing ties, wear long sleeved shirts that you can roll up. This will look nicer than a short-sleeved shirt and tie combination. You also have the option of wearing the blazer to work depending on the weather. If it is very hot, you do not have to keep wearing the blazer. You can carry it with you during the day and wear it occasionally in an air-conditioned building or at night when it is much cooler.

Work Attire for Women

You can wear colors such as white, blue, red, pink, and orange. These will work for your formal wear. You can wear polyester or rayon blend blouses, which will match very nicely with the suits.

Wearing suits in an office environment is very acceptable for women. These could be a pair of pants and a blazer with a nice silk blouse. You could wear a nice skirt along with the blazer. However, you would not need to wear a tie. You can buy the suits that cater to young women. These stores will fit you better and often have matching shirts to go with them.

You should not wear clothes that are too revealing. People consider these to be too risqué and do not belong in the office environment. Colleagues and other office personnel will make bad comments about you. Other things to avoid are cheap looking clothes. Typically, these are too rigid, which makes them uncomfortable. You should wear conservative black business shoes instead of high heels. These are acceptable in the office and are more comfortable.

For more ideas, you can attend fashion shows for business attire. Department stores and other organizations will host these fashion shows for women. You can find information in the local newspaper and the internet. Otherwise, you can get help from the stores and slowly build up your wardrobe.

The main thing to remember in wearing suits is that it must fit your body well. The suit should not be too tight or too loose fitting. You will not look good in either case. In the end, you may actually dispose of the suit and keep buying new ones. Try to bring a friend with good fashion taste and ideas. If you do not feel comfortable with the suit, wait the next week and see if you still want to buy it.

Casual Attire for Women

You do not have to wear the blazer all the time. If your profession calls for it, then make sure you have a very light cotton or linen type blazer. This will be much cooler for you in the summer. As an example, you may be used to wearing only jeans. As it turns out, you could be very beautiful in a flowing skirt and even more comfortable.

Wear jeans and simple blouses for casual wear. Cotton is very comfortable for the summer and easier to clean. You can wear color pastels in the summer for both blouses and t-shirts. You can match these tops with white pants or skirts, which look very well on women.

You should not wear short pants or very short skirts for work even if you have casual Fridays. You should still adhere to your own personal dress code. You would want to maintain an air of dignity at work.

In the fall and winter seasons, go into the heavier cottons and even wool clothes. Wear layers of clothing to help keep you warm. Turtleneck sweaters worn under blazers are acceptable in a professional work environment. You will look very nicely in this combination and it will help keep you from catching colds.

You should buy a wool overcoat for your office work environment. The overcoat not only keeps you warm but also looks very professional. Remember to wear layers of clothes to help keep your body warmth. You can also wear the overcoat on top of casual clothes. Do not wear very cheap looking winter coats made of mostly of polyester or nylon. These do not provide the needed protection from the cold air. It also does not give you a nice look for the office.

Hairstyles for Men and Women

The next thing that people notice about you is your hairstyle. Picking a look for you can also be very difficult since you need to be able to reproduce what a hair salon will do to your hair. Watch very carefully on how they use the brush and hairdryers on you. You need to know the motions so you can style your new hair cut as the salon had done.

Get a hairstyle that works for you. Each person will have certain hair thickness. They could be straight or curly. The stylist will know what works best if you do not have an idea. Look at the magazines they have for a hairstyle that looks appealing to you. Remember you can also change salons if you are not satisfied with your hair.

Ask questions on what shampoo, conditioners, and styling gel they use on you. Purchase these items from the salon for now so that you can try doing the style yourself at home the next day. Because you have to style your hair at home, pick a haircut that is simple for you.

Go to a reputable hair salon in the beginning. You may have to spend more money the first few times just to get the feel of it. Later you can find a lesser expensive place where you can tell them exactly what you want. Do not be afraid to tell the stylist what you want done to your hair. Typically, you should go once a month to get your haircut. Do not spend too much money for your haircut and style. Watch your budget because this is a monthly expense for you.

Extra advice for the men, do not shave your head. This look is not readily acceptable in a work environment. A shaved head comes across that you belong in gang or could be a troublemaker. You would not want this type of preconception put on you.

Wearing Eyeglasses for Men and Women

If you wear glasses, get either plastic or wire frames. However, do not buy thick plastic frames. Buy glasses that have rectangular shaped frames. Try to stay away from oval and especially circular shaped lenses. Do not buy large sized lenses. These look very awkward and do not fit anybody's face. Get lenses that are sleek looking and roughly about one inch tall. They are very comfortable and light on the bridge of your nose. The best lenses to get are the transition type, which get darker in the sunlight. This way, you would not have to buy sunglasses or clip-on sun shades for your glasses.

Colognes and Perfumes

The advices in this section are the same for both men and women. Wear colognes and perfumes that have a relatively light good scent. If you are not sure what to get, you can try common type colognes or perfumes in the magazine insets. Open it up and rub it on your wrist. Let it set and see if you like it. You can also try samples from the store department's display areas. Ask for assistance with the salespeople. They will give good advice on which scent will be appropriate for you. You could also ask your brother or sister for their opinions on some scents.

You should buy a small bottle first to ensure if you really like it. This way you will not waste your money. Just spray a small amount on your wrists or neck area. You could also spray into the air just in front of you and then walk through it. Do not spray too much on yourself. It will be too overbearing and make people uncomfortable around you.

Dining Advice for Men and Women

When it comes to food, you can read magazines dedicated to food and wine. This will be helpful when you go out to dine. Read your local city guide magazines for the reviews and recommendations on restaurants. Study and memorize how the magazines use the appropriate words to describe the food and wine. Learn all the small nuances that come in appreciating the taste of regional cooking. Expand your knowledge on different cuisines on how to eat them and the appropriate wines that go with them.

You should watch television shows specializing on preparing food. They are entertaining and very educational. Try to watch as many shows as you can on different types of cuisines. Once you learn how to prepare the food, you can then go out and visit restaurants that serve these foods. You can think of it as research, which you could do once a month.

If you find a good restaurant you like, visit it many times. Try as many dishes you can over time. This way you get a working knowledge of the food and culture. Go periodically until you become a regular and they know you there. This way when you do bring friends or a date for the first time, you are more relaxed. You will know what to order from the menu and you can help describe them to your friends or date.

Do not forget to wear casual and comfortable clothing when going out. Try to stay away from trends and fads. You can wear a nice black t-shirt with casual suits. Always wear casual shoes even with jeans and not gym shoes. Reserve the gym shoes for your sports activities. You must portray a successful and fun image to your friends and date. If you do prefer wearing jeans, try them with a black blazer. What is even better is a leather blazer. This is a classic look that will not fade away.

Speaking Advice for Men and Women

Language and your speech mannerism are also very important. Speak clearly and use proper grammar. If you need additional help, you can take speech classes in a community college. The courses are inexpensive and fun. This will be very helpful to you at the workplace should you have to do an oral presentation.

Practice speaking at home with a loud clear voice. You can record your speech with either a video or an audio recorder. You can then review your speech and make any necessary adjustments. You can observe your behavior and mannerism in the video. If you cannot see any bad habits, ask a friend to comment on your video. They will be able to give you objective suggestions on what you need to improve.

You can even buy an English language audio course. This course takes you through the language as a beginner. It shows you how to say the words properly and with the correct diction.

Other things that will help expand your vocabulary are reading books and magazines. Go to a library for suggestions or subscribe to a magazine. Practice using what you have learned in conversations. If you do not understand a word, look it up in a dictionary.

Watch well-known movies and listen very carefully on how the actors speak. Imitate a few key phrases and practice at home whenever you can. There is no shame in trying to improve your speech by talking loudly at home.

When driving in your car, you can also repeat back what the announcers are saying. This gives you a lot of time to practice. Try even singing with some of the songs. It is another way to keep practicing and exercising your mouth and vocal cords. You should be able to feel and hear the difference after a few months.

Dancing and Fitness for Men and Women

You must learn how to dance various steps for all the different types of night-clubs. Being a good dancer is also another way to dispel any stereotypical behaviors. When people see you dancing with rhythm they start to see beyond the color of the skin. They actually start to think of you in a different manner. Do not dance wildly about. Maintain grace and style. Men and women admire this most in any type of dance in all the nightclubs.

Take ballroom dancing in community colleges and private dance studios. This is also a good way to meet other people and network around should you need to change jobs. Do not be intimidated because you think that you are too uncoordinated to dance. There is no such thing. Do not be self-conscious of what you are doing. Do not listen to friends or family that will make fun of you. They are probably just as scared of dancing and are jealous of you. They themselves do not know the joy of dancing.

You also will need to build up your body. Take up tennis and volleyball for recreation and endurance. You do not have to become a professional player but enough to play well. By doing this, you get the needed exercise and a better outlook in life. It helps you get out of the house and to interact with many people. You can also take up some classes if you want to become better. This will help you learn how to play with form.

At the same time, become a member in a fitness class. You can use the various machines such as a stationary bicycle and a treadmill to increase your stamina. Take up weight lifting with free weights for upper body strength. Focus on doing repetitions rather than adding more and more weights. Use a goal of being able to do twenty-five comfortably and then add weights that will bring it back down to ten. As your number of repetitions increase, then add more weights and repeat the process. This will give you a more sculptured body, which will improve your appearance. Your sports activity will even become better. There will be more power behind your tennis game. You will not get sick as much.

You will realize that as you improve your body, mind and soul you become more independent. You will not rely as much on what other people think. People will perceive a change in your mannerism. Nobody will be able to intimidate you. People will realize that you are stronger than they are. You can disagree with them and point out their poor behavior towards Asians and other ethnic people. They will come to terms that they cannot affect your mind.

12

Skin Care

Commercial Products

Skin care can be a very serious topic for many people. Not too many Asian people are aware that acne and pimples are treatable professionally. If you have oily skin and periodically breakout, do not buy any cleansing pads or facial soaps from the pharmacy. These do not really work and you will just be wasting a lot of money. You will become frustrated and discouraged as the months go by where you still breakout.

Perpetual skin blemishes that appear on your face can lower your self-esteem. You feel very self-conscious and do not want to go to many social events. You feel ashamed of how you look and sometimes feel out of place where ever you go. Not too many people find these types of skin condition attractive at all. In fact, children who do not have any respect for anyone may ridicule you.

There are products constantly sold over the counter that claim to prevent acne and other blemishes. You will see major telemarketing advertisements on television about using facial crèmes and lotion that will prevent breakouts. These claim to be able to heal your facial skin condition. Remember that everything you are watching is one big drawn out commercial. You know that as commercial goes, sometimes the truth is exaggerated. The claims being made are most likely from paid actors. There are even commercials where well known actors endorse these products.

Do not be swayed with famous actors that are promoting some sort of acne lotions. These products can be very expensive and will require you to keep purchasing them in order to clear up your face. Yes, you will find it hard to resist when you have a facial skin condition. You want to have an instant cure to help you look better so that you can lead a normal life. You want to buy the product and hope that it will help clear up your face.

You want to listen to the advertisement because you are not educated enough about your skin condition. You may feel that you also do not want people to know that you are seeking help and treatment. You just want to go to a pharmacy and get any brand lotion on the shelf. No matter what your friends and family tell you, do not buy these products.

Professional Help for Men and Women

The best step to take is to make an appointment with a dermatologist. It is much better to see a professional to diagnose your skin condition. By going through these steps, you will understand why you are having the acne and pimples. You will find that these are treatable as diseases and can be cured with prescription medicine. These medicines are very strong and you must follow the doctor's instructions.

The whole process can take a few months depending on your level of acne. You must be patient about the treatment. Nothing will happen overnight. The prescription medicine can be expensive but could be covered by your health insurance. You should really check with your health care provider first before going to the doctor. The medicines can reach into the hundreds of dollars but is worth the cure.

Listen to what your dermatologist has to recommend and continue the sessions. The doctor would invariably prescribe a strong medicine that you have to take daily. However, your face will start to feel dryer and a little smoother. You will see great improvements in your skin within a few months. The breakouts will actually stop forming.

If you are happy with the results just from taking the medicine, then that may be all that you will need. You can then go on with your life with a new outlook. The best thing you can do is get the treatment as soon as possible before it gets worse.

Should you have children, you must take them right away to see a dermatologist. They must be treated before it gets worse as they mature, especially going through the puberty phase. Having acne and pimples do interfere with your children's schoolwork and outlook. They will become frustrated and possibly even depressed because of their constant breakouts. They can become withdrawn and not lead a normal healthy childhood. Therefore, you must look after your children's skin condition also. Remember that the treatment could be covered by your health insurance.

Depending on the severity of your skin facial condition, the next step to help give you a better-looking facial skin will be a chemical peel. This procedure burns off the top layers of your skin. You will get a burning sensation as it is applied onto your face. It can be painful as it is being applied, depending on the chemical strength. However, rest assured that it would be worth the sacrifice when you stop breaking out and start having a smoother skin.

The bad effect of the chemical peel is the scabs that result from the chemical burn. This is temporary and will last for three to four weeks. However, the important thing is that a new smooth layer of skin is forming under the scab. The whole scab area will feel very uncomfortable but is worth all the pain. Once the scab starts to dry up and fall off, you can see your new beautiful skin.

This whole procedure is worth the discomfort and temporary scab look on your face because you will get a smoother looking skin. Any small blemishes such as blackheads in your face will be taken off. Even your forehead could be smoothed out a bit. You will have great looking skin after the chemical peel.

Do not listen to people making fun of you when they see the scabs. Pay no attention to them. They do not understand about respecting other people's conditions and feelings. The scab look is temporary and once it is gone, you will look great.

Once you have finished the chemical peel, do not suntan anymore. You will have a new layer of skin that will be very sensitive. You will look younger to your friends and loved ones. Do not throw away what you have gained from all your sacrifices. Always try to cover your face whenever you go out. You must wear a hat that will shield your face from the sun or carry an umbrella.

Some doctors can actually give you lower levels of chemical peel so that you do not have a large scab on your face. However, you will have to go several times in order to expose the young skin beneath. This longer method may not have the full effect of exposing the young skin. This method may be best for someone who does not have a more severe acne case or pimples.

You should also see a dermatologist for varicose veins in your legs. The doctor can slowly treat them until they are gone. The varicose veins can slow down your walking pace and can be painful. What happens is that blood flow is hampered. The one thing to remember is that it is treatable.

The same advice holds should you have a bump anywhere, which could be a cyst underneath the skin. See a doctor about it immediately. Removing the cyst should be a real simple procedure. You should be out of the office in about an hour.

You can also remove unwanted moles from your face. The doctor may use minor surgery or a laser procedure. Either method will obviously leave some scabs but they will be very small. It should heal up in a few weeks.

Do not try other types of treatment such as facial mud and food product types of lotion without consulting your dermatologist. Your doctor will know what is best for you and will help you. Your doctor will tell you if these products will be able to help you or not. The same advice applies should you want to try very expensive facial soaps that advertise better-looking skin, even if famous people endorse these products.

Avoiding the Sun

If you have perfect skin, then you are very fortunate. You must take very good care of your skin by moisturizing and keeping it clean. Do not stay too long in the sunlight. No matter how well you can get a tan, always use a sunscreen lotion. Try to avoid staying out too long in the sunlight. Do not take any chances of getting skin cancer. If you see any slight blemish, see a doctor immediately.

The suntan that you thought would look great on you will actually do more damage in the future. The sun will accelerate your aging process. Your skin will become dried up as you tan more and more. You can see all these effects with people who are constantly sun tanning every chance they get. So many people actually look much older than they are. Because of this, you must always protect yourself from the sunlight.

You must try not to go on vacations where there are beaches. It is too tempting for you to lie down and enjoy the sun. You must try to stay under an umbrella or an outdoor café with a roof. If you must go out into the sun, you must put on the proper clothing to cover your body and face. Always put on some sun lotion with the proper strength. Even if your skin is the dark type already, put on a heavy rated lotion to protect your skin.

You must also wear a nice looking hat to protect your face. You can also carry a small umbrella that will give you the proper shade. If you do not have any of these things, just put a t-shirt or towel over your head and face. No matter what your decision, get out of the sun as soon as possible.

Having too much sun also has another bad effect. It will dry up your skin and can give you spots. Your skin will lose its elasticity and healthy glow. You will get blemishes called sunspots. These are the round brown colored discoloration in your skin. You will also notice that you will get much more wrinkles everywhere. The majority can be seen in your eyes and chin. Even at a young age, you will experience this wrinkling effect. The worse thing is that the wrinkling effect is irreversible.

Once the doctor has cured you of acne, blemishes, and other skin conditions, you must take all the advice to heart and protect your skin. You must not stay in the sunlight for long periods. You may actually have to stop lying on beaches trying to get a tan. This is a fact. You would not want to get skin cancer and get very old looking skin.

Lotions and Chemicals

During the winter season, always use lotion on your hands. This will keep the skin from drying up too much. Wear gloves whenever you go outside even for short distances. In addition, keep your face protected from the cold wind by wearing a scarf or bandana. This will help ensure you have great healthy looking hands and face. You must also do these things for your children.

You can wear wool if you do not get an allergic reaction or become easily irritated. If you do, you can wear layers of thick cotton or synthetic clothes to keep you warm. This way you do not get any skin rashes from your winter clothes. This holds true for any types of clothes. You should wear clothes that do not give you any skin discomfort. Usually the best things to wear are plain loose fitting cotton clothes.

You must be careful whenever you use cleaning chemicals at home. Protect your hands by wearing cleaning gloves. You would not want to have direct skin contact with powerful cleaners. These could be oven cleaners and disinfectants. Even the fumes could affect your breathing and possible have a long lasting effect on your lungs.

If you do touch the chemicals with your hands, be sure to wash them thoroughly. Try to time your cleaning after preparing any food. This way you do not have to touch any raw food that you will be cooking. The reason is that there may be chemical residue that could get into the food you are cooking. You and your family will then ingest the contaminated food.

When you have finished cleaning with chemicals, try to avoid preparing food at all. Do not also use your hands to touch the food to place into your mouth. There still may be some chemical residue on your hands. Never touch your eyes also because they can become irritated and injured. The same goes for your children and babies. Do not handle them unless you have thoroughly washed your hands. You will contaminate your babies with the chemicals on your hands.

13

Health and Fitness

Preparing and Eating Food

Your health is the most important thing. It is more important than money, popularity or fame. Without good health, you will not be able to do many things you enjoy. You will not be able to play tennis or go dancing. Staying healthy should be a full time job for you.

You must be always aware of how your body reacts to certain types of food. Try to remember what you have eaten whenever you feel sick. It could be that you may be having an allergic reaction. Always eat good food and plenty of vegetables. Being Asian, you undoubtedly have white rice as a basic staple diet.

Eating steamed white rice helps fill you up. It helps prevent you from eating only meat for lunch or dinner. The reason is you usually end up using a one to one ratio of rice and the main meat dish. The rice and the other vegetables in the food is an automatic buffer so that you do not eat too much with beef.

Whenever you have to travel for work or change jobs, always look for a Chinese or other Asian restaurants. It is a good idea to drive around but sometimes the phone book will be more helpful. These restaurants will serve all the rice dishes you would need for lunch and dinner. You can ask someone to help if you cannot find one by yourself.

You must try to minimize eating in fast food restaurants. You should not eat too much greasy foods such as deep fried chicken and hamburgers. In particular, when you are eating chicken, you must discard the chicken skins. It may be tasty with all the spices and everything, but it is not very healthy. The chicken skin has so much fat that it will make you overweight. You will be more susceptible to heart problems.

Whenever you are eating beef or pork, always trim the fat off and put it on the side of your plate. Do not eat the fat. You must never eat the fat no matter how tempting it is. It is well known that it can also contribute to health problems.

Also, do not use salt at all when eating, but rather use pepper. There are enough salt in today's foods that you do not need to add anymore.

You do not have to become a vegetarian in order to eat healthy food. You do not need any special diet where you will have to buy diet powders or drinks. All you have to do is eat in moderation. Do not overindulge whenever you have lunch or dinner. It is all right to eat dessert pastries once in awhile, although fresh fruits are better.

If you are watching your weight, there are certain foods that you should not eat. These are nuts, cheese (includes pizza), potato chips, fries, donuts, candies, bacon, and ice cream. You should also not drink regular milk every night because it is equivalent to eating five strips of bacon. Instead, drink the low fat or the 2% skim milk.

Also, do not use sugar and cream in your coffee and tea. Drinking it straight will be better. Do not drink fruit flavored drinks that are loaded with sugar. These will just contribute to your weight gain.

Do not drink excessive amounts of alcohol, especially hard liquor. Do not habitually take medicines and pills for small minor things. You will get addicted to them. These are never good to keep on using. Do not smoke cigarettes or use any other tobacco products. Nothing good ever comes out of it. Always keep the thought of getting cancer in your mind.

When you cook at home always, keep your utensils clean. Wash your hands after handling meats and even eggs. The reason is that if you do not, you will be touching things in your kitchen where you could be spreading the germs.

Use a plastic type cutting board because it can be better cleaned of bacteria. Thoroughly wash the knives and cutting board after using it with chicken and meat. Keep all the countertops clean. You can use ordinary soap and water and scrub it clean. The same goes for the sink so always clean it up after a heavy wash.

Do not keep leftovers in the refrigerator over two days, no matter what. They can make you sick. Just throw away the leftovers rather than guessing if it is still good to eat. Some foods just do not keep well. Try to cook smaller amounts of food so that you do not end up with leftovers. This will be better for your diet and health. Moreover, whenever you bring out the food, you expose it to more germs in the room. The nutrition value also goes down anyway as you reheat a food multiple times.

Do not buy a lot of raw chicken, meat, fish, and pork where you place it in the freezer for future use. You may be doing this in trying to save money from the sales. Remember, some of these have deadlines when they should be used even if they are frozen. When you do defrost the various meats, it takes some time and gets messy. Do not buy so many of these things where they may just expire in your refrigerator or cupboard. You would have saved nothing if you threw them.

Do not be afraid to throw out old frozen meats and other bottled goods from your refrigerator. You must dispose of any expired items even if they still look good in appearance to you. These old food items can give you food poisoning. You are not saving any money if you end up very sick in the hospital. You can always buy the items again when you do need them.

It is much better to buy the meat, chicken or fish from the grocery store on the day you are going to prepare it. By doing it this way, you are using fresh meat that is already soft. All you would have to do is season it and cook it. There is less fuss and mess. You freezer is also freed up from overcrowding.

Do not throw raw or leftover foods directly into the garbage cans. These will breed bacteria in the trash. Whenever you have to throw the raw chicken bones or fish parts, use the small plastic bags you received from the grocery stores. The bag does not have to be fully loaded. Tie the bag ends together and then you can place it inside your main kitchen tall garbage bags. You must do the same thing for any food refuse coming from the dining table.

For used oil or grease in the frying pan, pour it into an old bottle or a small plastic bag, which you can then throw into your garbage can. You are containing the grease in a much more manageable way. Do not pour any oil and grease into the sink. This will clog up your drain very fast and even possibly your sewer system.

You must always wash your hands whenever you touch your garbage can. This especially goes for your children who do not know well enough to stay away from the trash. Make sure you wash their hands every time you see them touch the lid or edge of your trashcan. Remember that they have a habit of always putting their fingers in their mouths.

By doing the things listed above, your main garbage can will not have any food products either raw or cooked exposed to the room. It will help minimize or even prevent bacteria and germs from growing in the garbage can. This is a more sanitary way to live especially if you have children. Your house will also have a cleaner smell. You will not have that musky smell of old food sitting in the trash at room temperature.

If your garbage can has a slight odor, spray it immediately with a cleaner. Take it outside and spray it down with your hose. You can use regular dishwasher soap and thoroughly clean it. If there is still a lingering smell, just throw away your trashcan and get a brand new one. The cost of having a healthier home environment is minimal compared to hospital bills.

You must always clean the toilet and bathroom thoroughly. This is an area where many germs will grow. Spray everything with bathroom cleaner. Throw away all the used paper towels in small plastic bags, which you can tie, shut.

Keep your toothbrush as far away from the toilet as possible. The reason is that whenever you flush, there are mists of contaminated water shooting up. The airborne water particles will easily settle down onto your exposed toothbrush. This will then become a breeding ground for germs, which you then insert into your mouth.

Working Out

You can take many sports to stay fit. The key thing is to have a good calisthenics program. You must have a weekly workout to keep your heart healthy. You can take up running, walking, bicycling and even aerobics. If you prefer to workout indoors, you can join a health and fitness club of your choice. These clubs are worth the membership fees you have to pay. You can shop around to get the best prices on the annual fees. Look for a club that is having a grand opening because they usually offer discounted rates.

Do not buy any exercise and fitness machines to have at home. Usually these end up becoming clothes hangers. These equipments will just sit there collecting dusts. Some of these machines are treadmills, stationary bicycles, and abdominal machines. At home, it is hard to try to have a good workout. There is no motivation to make you use the equipment. Sometimes you become distracted with house chores and family members visiting.

They also take up so much space in your house. Some of these are very bulky and can actually be dangerous. You could hurt yourself while exercising and nobody will be there to help. Your children can also hurt themselves on the equipment because they think it is a plaything. On the other hand, they could just be trying to imitate what you were doing.

Do not buy any electronic belts that shock your muscles. Do not buy any salves or other fat reducing lotions to rub on your body. There is no quick solution to loosing weight with lotions. You will just be wasting your money.

The best thing is still to go to the health clubs. Once you get inside, you are motivated to exercise. You will not be distracted from having a great workout. The various stair, bicycle, and running machines are great for the calisthenics. If you are using machines for the first time, ask for assistance with the personnel. You may even want to have a personal trainer in the beginning.

The fitness trainer will show you how to operate the machines so that you do not get hurt. They will also give you a set schedule on which you must follow. The schedule is designed around your current health and physical ability. The machines settings will get higher as you progress. The reason is that the workout becomes too easy where your body is not challenged enough.

The key is to spend at least thirty minutes on one machine and then go to a different one. You can even switch back and forth between machines during a session. For example, you can use the treadmill for about thirty minutes. Then switch to a bicycle for another thirty minutes. After that, you go back to the treadmill or another type of machine. This way you do not get bored easily. You also get a chance to relax the first set of muscles from using the first machine.

Always use the machine setting where you are comfortable. You should not be experiencing any pain when you use the machines. You should not be strained where you are running out of breath or having dizzy spells. Keep yourself hydrated by drinking enough water as you workout.

You can also take aerobics on a weekly basis. This will help tone your body more while you gain stamina. Do not be shy about taking the classes. However, go for the beginner's class first. You will find this easier and not hurt yourself. The aerobics will become easier with time.

After a few months, your heart rate will be lower. This is a good indication that you are becoming healthier. When you are at this stage, you should start exercising with weights. This will give you more strength and a sculptured body. You can use some of the machine weights and the free weights for this next step in your overall workout.

You will hear that weight lifting will make you too bulky. This is not the case. By lifting light dumb bells, you will be toning your body more. The key is to focus on the amount of repetitions and not on putting heavier weights. Try to target doing ten repetitions, which is one set. Rest about a minute or so and then do another set. Repeat this about for about four to five sets.

When you can achieve twenty to twenty-five repetitions on the first set, then you can start to add more weights. This should bring you back down to ten sets again in the beginning of your set. The time where you add more weights should take months, so do not worry if you think you are not progressing fast enough.

Developing strength in weight lifting cannot be rushed. Be patient when you start going into the program. The great thing is that you will have great strength in your arms and legs. You will also find that some of your clothes may not fit anymore. This is normal and you should be very happy. It is an indication that your workout routine is working.

Always wear comfortable clothes in the fitness club. Bring a small towel to put down on the benches when you use the machines. This will keep you from touching somebody else's sweat and bacteria. Do not lie down on the floor of the fitness club. Everybody walks on that surface with his or her shoes. You will be lying on a bed of germs, which can give you a rash on your back.

Do not take any protein drink that is sold at the health club and nutrition stores. Some of these drinks have a lot of sugar and usually have to be mixed with milk. This is not a good thing to drink. It will make you fat rather than help you develop proper muscles. You will be spending a lot of money on the protein drink and still not feel any stronger.

The best thing for good muscle development is to eat properly and focus on the repetitions. As you add more weights, it will help increase your strength and muscles. It just depends on how big you really want to become. However, do not overdo the workout. You can end up hurting yourself and possibly doing some permanent damage to your body.

If the health club has a Jacuzzi or swimming pool, do not use it. You will see that all sorts of people use it. There are children, teenagers and senior citizens. Remember, the children could be using them as toilets. In addition, you do not know if the other people have any skin conditions that can be contagious. The pools could be just full of swirling germs.

Cleanliness

Always wash your hands thoroughly with soap after your workout. You have touched many machines where other people have used them. You do not want to get bacteria from somebody else's hands. Remember, the health club is a place where everyone is sweating from their workouts. They are all wiping down their sweat with towels, which they handle with their hands. Some people who have a cold also continue to exercise in the health club. Therefore, as they sneeze or cough onto their hands, they spread their germs onto the equipment. This is a fact, which is why health clubs request that you wipe down the equipment you have finished using.

In fact, wash your hands always before leaving the bathroom in any public places. These places include your workplace, restaurants, gas stations, malls, churches, and other office buildings. You do not know whether the previous person who used the facility actually washed their hands. Some people actually do not wash their hands at all after using the washroom.

When you either see a sick person at work or in any public place, try hard not to touch anything they have touched. People typically blow their nose and will get germs on their hands. In addition, if they have not washed their hands, you will catch the cold from contact. Avoid the area where someone would have sneezed or coughed. There are germs flying in that area. It is best to let it settle down and then you can go through that area.

14

Social Dancing

Learning Salsa Dancing

Social dancing is a great way to relax and get some exercise. You should learn Salsa and Cha-cha because these forms of dances are fun and very rewarding. It teaches you poise and proper behavior in a social gathering with friends. You will not become anxious should there be dancing involved, especially in weddings. You will be more confident and sure of yourself.

The best places to go dancing these steps are in Latin clubs that cater to Salsa dancers. These clubs do exist in just about every city. Sometimes you may have to drive far away but it usually is worth the trip. Some people will drive over an hour just to be able to dance. You can look in the phone book and the internet to find these Latin clubs. You will find different types of nightclubs that play Salsa music.

If you are a young man or woman, knowing how to dance Salsa and Cha-cha will put you above the rest of the crowd. When they see you dancing and having a lot of fun, they think of you in a different light. Dancing is a type of art form where you can express your feelings and show your artistic style. When you have gone through dance classes and mastered the techniques, you start forming your own patterns. You will then set yourself apart from the other people dancing. There will be times you will be asked where you learned the moves.

In fact, you will be dancing all night with many different partners. For the men, the phrase "Would you like to dance?" is one of the best icebreakers in these nightclubs. Many women really love to dance and are not shy to accept a well-proposed question. You will never run out of dance partners. There will be occasions too that women will ask you to dance when they see how good of a dancer you are.

As for the women, you will always be asked by the men to dance with them. Especially when they see how well you can dance Salsa. The men are there to dance and so you can be assured you will be able to practice your steps.

You must remember that all the good dancers with form have taken lessons. You cannot learn true Salsa dancing in your sleep. Dancing Salsa is similar to playing tennis. You can hit the ball back and forth over the net. However, to engage in a real tennis game requires more from you. You will need to know how to: position your body; grip the tennis racket; and how to swing the tennis racquet. You get this knowledge from taking lessons and not from watching people. You will also need to practice the motions repeatedly on your own until it becomes second nature to you. There will be no time to try to remember what you have learned during an actual tennis match. All the actions are taking place within seconds of each other.

This is the same with dancing Salsa and Cha-cha. The main point here is that you must take dancing lessons to learn Latin dancing. The Salsa and Cha-cha requires you to know the eight count in the music. This is where you have to keep your timing of your patterns and rhythm on the beat. You may not get this until about one to two months later so do not be discouraged.

The reason is that you need to feel the music but this will take time. You must practice the count just about every night along with all the patterns. The steps in the patterns must fall in specific beats. In addition, as in any activity that you practice, you are very conscious of the steps and of what you are doing. You are thinking ahead and trying to remember the steps. You are learning numerous rules and techniques from the teacher. You need continuously practice the patterns in their original count and place. This form of dancing cannot be just thrown together where you can flail your hands about. You will actually hurt the other people dancing on the floor.

You will eventually memorize the steps and know the beat of the music. Your steps will become smoother and you will hit the patterns critical point on each beat. This is where you will look great to other people because the patterns and steps you are doing are in time with the music. You also start to dance from the heart and with the music. Your moves stop becoming erratic as you go through one set of pattern into another. Moreover, you learn how to accentuate your moves with the music.

In dancing, always start slow and do the basic moves. As the music approaches the middle part of the song, this is where the tempo is getting more intense and the instrumental part happens. At which point, you and your partner can separate from each other to do freestyle footwork. Towards the end of the music, the climax is approaching. Now you can throw in the more complex moves and intricate patterns. At the very end, you and your partner can perform a dip that really accents the whole dance both of you just accomplished.

Latin Club Atmosphere

The Latin club's atmosphere is quite different from the techno type of music. The techno type nightclubs have people who continuously play games among themselves. The women are all going to play hard to get and will often refuse to dance. The men are all putting on an act of being very macho and are ready to start fights in order to impress the girls watching. You should stay away from these types of nightclubs because you could be caught in the middle of it all. You do not need this type of aggravation in your life.

You will see that these people do eventually end up just standing around the nightclub with drinks in their hands. The hours will go by which you really could have spent dancing. In addition, when the nightclub is starting to close, you will see some of the same men and women who have been playing games going home alone. This is no way for you spend your time in a nightclub.

The Latin clubs tend to have a more pleasing and relaxing atmosphere. Most of the regular people who go there are avid Salsa dancers and just want to dance. In actuality, not too many people drink alcohol in these clubs. They are really more focused on dancing. They are there to practice new turns and even learn more techniques. The experienced dancers can pick up new moves just from observing other people dancing.

Nightclub Attire for Men

If you are a man, wear nice casual looking clothes. The key here again is to wear comfortable clothes. You should wear a nice cotton type t-shirts under a blazer or suit ensemble. The best blazers to wear are the soft flowing type. Again, a black blazer should be your choice of color. It always looks good in any setting. When you are getting too warm, you should take off your blazer immediately so that you can cool down. During the summer, you could wear a casual black shirt with the sleeves rolled up. This always looks better in the nightclub than the white shirt you wear for work.

Nightclub Attire for Women

If you are a woman, you should also wear very comfortable clothes. Wear tasteful skirts because you will be doing a lot of spinning and turning. You would not want your skirt to fly up exposing your undergarments. You can also wear slacks with a nice blouse and blazer. Take the blazer off also, once you start to get too warm. As for the shoes, you must not wear open toe shoes because you can get seriously hurt. Men and women will step on you accidentally and it could be very painful. This is especially dangerous should a woman with high heels step on your foot where the pointed heel can break the skin.

Places to Learn Salsa

There are many places where you can take Salsa lessons. Community colleges will have programs teaching Salsa and other ballroom dancing. There are nightclubs that sponsor lessons very early in the evening. These are great to attend because you will learn more from these instructors and you will get plenty of practice time. You can also ask the instructor if they teach somewhere else. They will give you a schedule of other nightclubs where they teach during the week.

You must try to go to the other nightclubs for additional lessons. This will give you a chance to experience the other nightclubs and see how the other people there dance. The nightclubs will vary in their operations. Some will just require you to pay a minimum cover charge and the lessons will all be free. Other nightclubs will be free to get inside but you will be charged for the lessons. All these lessons will be worth the money you will have to spend.

Some instructors will even have studios where they hold regular classes. These are great to attend because you will get a more structured lesson. Be sure to continue going because the lessons will progress from beginners all the way to advance. You will be taught more patterns and techniques every session.

In the studio, the instructor will be able to give you more attention. There the steps can be broken down more for you. You can also watch yourself in the mirrors on how well you are performing the moves. In addition, just like in the nightclubs, you will always have partners if you cannot bring a friend. The instructor rotates the people so that everyone gets a chance to dance.

There is an annual dance event called the Salsa Congress held in San Juan, Puerto Rico. The whole focus is Salsa and nothing but Salsa. There are seminars during the day where instructors discuss the finer points of dancing and show several dance moves. Several instructors will talk making the seminars last for hours. They stay late also to answer many questions about the techniques and routines.

Later in the evening, a great dance hall is set up for the all the people who have signed up. Two stages are typically set up in the banquet hall. One stage is for the live band and the other is for invited performers from different countries. The dancers will perform the Salsa as performed in their respective country. In effect, they are showing their own unique styles of their respective regions.

If you are looking for something different in a vacation, sign up for the next Salsa Congress. You can easily find the information in the internet regarding the next one. This is actually a great vacation type you and your friends can attend. You can even enjoy this tour package with your spouse. There is food, music, sightseeing, and lots of dancing in stored for everyone.

Benefits of Salsa Dancing

You are learning to dance an elegant dance form and will be meeting new people. You could think of your lessons as another way to network. There will be different people with different work backgrounds. Who knows, you may meet someone who could help you find a job or even become a partner for a business venture. You could even become romantically involved with someone from the Salsa club. Remember, the atmosphere there is quite different from the techno type clubs.

In dancing Salsa, you will be getting a good and relaxing type of workout. You will be on your feet for hours just dancing the night away. The usual rigid walls around people are not present in the Salsa nightclubs. People from different ethnic backgrounds go dancing in the Latin club. The Latin clubs are unique in a way that everyone who dances formal Salsa has certain respect for each other.

You may even get addicted to dancing Salsa and start entering local nightclub contests. Beginner dancers and even intermediate enter the contests for fun. Everybody in the Salsa club will cheer for all the dancers because many are repeat patrons that go there. They know how hard it is to learn the dance and more importantly, how it could bring many people together. You should definitely enter the contest if you have a steady dance partner. It does help to know your partner because not everyone takes Salsa lessons to dance. The other contestants may actually have regular partners.

Even if you are not very serious about dancing, at least learn how to dance Salsa very well. Practice at home every week by yourself and with a partner. It will also get you out of the house where you can meet other people. You will find that there will be people out there always looking for dance partners especially for lessons. You and a partner must practice until you two have absolutely memorized the routines.

The reason for the advice in learning how to dance is that you will be able to use the moves and routines in other dance forms. For example, the majority of the Salsa moves can be used in Cha-cha and even Swing. The various routines and moves all blend very well into the other music. You will never get bored or just stand around whenever you are in any type of nightclub once you master Salsa.

Another reason why you should master dancing Salsa is that when you start traveling overseas, you will find Salsa clubs over there. There are followers of Salsa dancing in the other countries. Look in the travel books and the internet to find these clubs. You will be amazed that there are even regular clubs that play Latin music on certain nights in the other countries. In addition, even if you cannot speak the language, you can dance Salsa with great confidence. Your partner will understand your moves because they are rather universal. You will find that you will easily make friends once they see how well you can dance Salsa. You may even end up teaching them new moves.

Tango Dancing

Another great dance to learn when you have a chance is Tango. This dance is more intimate and exciting to watch. You and your partner move as one on the dance floor. Both of you have to know how to read each other's body. You go through the dance very majestically. Because of this, you should definitely have a steady partner when you go for the lessons. Here you can actually wear a very formal suit and evening dress. This is where you can put on your best jewelries and not worry about overdressing.

Although, there are not too many dance clubs that specifically play Tango, you should try it when you get a chance. This will limit your practice time for learning it, which is why you should definitely have a steady partner. At least some community colleges will offer the dance on their programs. You will also be able to find studios that teach Tango around any city. Ask your Salsa instructor about Tango. You may be lucky enough to find that the instructor can also teach Tango or may know someone who does. When you do start learning Tango, you must practice it at home periodically with a partner.

15

Dating

Being a Gentleman

You must always be a gentleman whenever you are out on a date with a woman. Women look for this trait in all the men. It does not matter whether you just met the woman or she is someone you have been seeing for a long time. Just because you have been with a girl for a long time does not mean you can start being wild and disrespectful to her. You must always respect her as if you two are meeting for the very first time.

You should open the doors for her at a restaurant, the car, and at home. You should help carry anything she may have in her hands. Be conscious of what you are saying whenever you two are having a conversation. You should be sensitive to her feelings. Listen intently to what she is saying and respect her opinions whenever she is speaking to you. This is a great chance for the two of you to know more about each other. Ask your date about her background and find out about her family.

Do not show off or be a braggart to your date. You do not need to impress your date with some trivial physical abilities or accomplishments. There is no benefit in doing so. You will just be making a fool of yourself. You should just be yourself and act naturally. Do not hide anything from your date. Let her know exactly what you are thinking and feeling. This will help you know further if your date would like to see you again. Be kind to your date and let your natural humor come out.

Whenever you take your date to go dancing, you must not look at anybody else. You should also not dance with other women and leave your date by herself. You must stay focused on your date. Do not flirt with other women around you, including the server. You must show your date great respect by giving her your full attention.

When you are taking your date home, make sure she gets inside her home safely. Do not drive away immediately. If you can see from your car, watch her go inside her home. If you feel like calling and think that, you are completely comfortable with your date, then go ahead and call her. If the feeling is mutual, then you are extremely lucky find someone.

If there does not seem to be any chemistry between you and your date, then you should not pursue her anymore. You will be wasting your time. You may actually miss the opportunity in meeting a woman who is more your type. Always know right away if you need to move on with your life. You can meet many more women out there.

Do not date a woman who likes a lot of expensive jewelry. These women may be after your money. Do not date a woman who swears a lot and gets angry very easily. Her anger will be directed to you at some point in time. Try to stay away from women who are too loose and like to date many men. You would be wasting your time with this type of woman. They could be very promiscuous and could pass a virus to you.

Do not date a woman who is very wild or shouts a lot. She can embarrass you in a restaurant if you two disagree on something. Try to stay away from women who cannot act ladylike, especially if she talks too loudly. You would not want to show to your family this type of women. If you are not comfortable of introducing a woman to friends and family, then this woman is definitely not for you.

You should stay with a woman that you really like. The two of you should be very comfortable with each other. You will find many opportunities where you can find out if the woman you are dating will make you happy. This is of course the ultimate goal for both of you.

Being a Lady

Conversely, if you are the woman on a date with someone, you should always act as a lady. Men look for this trait in all the women. Do not say anything that will embarrass your date. There is no need to try to humiliate your date. You should not compete with your date and try to make him feel unworthy. Pay close attention to your date when you two are out having dinner. When you go dancing, you should not dance with other men and leave your date alone. Never ever, flirt with other men, especially with the waiters and bartenders.

This is your chance to learn about your date. You can find out what he wants to do in life. You must find out about his career goals and if he is serious about making a living. You must never date a man who has very little ambition in life and work. Otherwise, you may become just like him if you do decide to be with him. Your training from childhood and your hard work in college will be suppressed because of him.

Do not become romantically involved with inconsiderate men. You may think you are attracted to a rebel, but in reality you getting involved with a disrespectful man. You will only become involved with someone who could actually be dishonest. These types of men would eventually become violent and could even start hitting you. You must stay away from these types of men.

Observe how the man talks about his family, especially with his mother. This will give you a general indication of how he might treat you. You would not want to marry a man who will not be a supportive husband and who will not give you the proper respect. If you do, you will eventually get divorced as your eyes slowly open up again. You can avoid all this if you act decisively.

Do not get involved with a man who will go out socially without you. This is a sure sign that he is not ready to be romantically involved to one woman. This man could actually be playing around and loves to see other women. They will lie about anything just to get to you.

Do not sell yourself short to any man. Remember that you have your own mind and are strong. Never allow yourself to be involved with a man who will not help you grow. You will become involved in a meaningless relationship and will waste your time. The uncaring man will actually stunt your intellectual and professional growth. He will give you many reasons to give up your career and to stay home to care for him. This is no way for you to live.

Never date a man who is not a gentleman. If the man does not like to spend money for a nice dinner, this may be an indication for you to drop him. He could be someone who does not hold a nice job. He could latch onto you just for your money where you would have to support him. Alternatively, he may not have any real interest in you at all.

Wear appropriate clothing and dress for the occasion. Do not wear too wild looking clothes or very dull old clothes. This is not very attractive to men. Always make sure you already have nice clothes in your wardrobe before going on a date. You must be very comfortable but also look nice. Never wear any type of athletic shoes. You can wear either very formal shoes or nice semi-formal. Again this depends on where both of you are going for the date.

Dinner Date for Men and Women

For the very first date, both of you should really make it semi-formal. The reason is both you and your date will have to make some effort to look nice for each other. Both of you will be more relaxed and can really enjoy each other's company. You can go to a coffee shop or a pastry shop where it is relaxing.

Going formal on the first date is not advisable. There are too many things you will have to schedule. If you wanted to go to a formal restaurant, you will have to make a reservation. You would not want to arrive there without any reservations. You could be turned away or you could both wait over an hour for your table. This makes for a very bad first date. Moreover, you and your date will start to get very hungry and become uncomfortable.

Never go to a very popular and crowded place. There are so many people talking that you will not be able to hear each other. You will be shouting over the food in order to have a conversation. You dinner can also come late because of all the people that are being serviced. You will not get the attention you would like from the waiters. You might even be rushed by the servers in finishing your meal in order to clear your table for the next set of customers.

When you two are going to have dinner, order a simple food that is easy to eat. Do not order food where you will have to do a lot of work to eat it. It is very distracting. Do not order anything that will get your hands dirty. For example, ordering a steamed lobster or shrimp with shells means that you will have to use your hands to take off the shells. Your hands will get dirty and the seafood smell will stay on your hands. You will divide your attention on trying to eat your food while trying to look good to your date. You also should stay away from eating salads because of the tiny bits of green leaves that could be stuck in your teeth.

Order something that is easy to eat because you would want to have a good conversation. You need to keep your mouth clear of food in order to speak properly. A breaded boneless chicken type of dish would be a great main course to order. It will be very easy to cut and eat. You can cut it into small pieces so that you do not have a lot of food inside your mouth. This meat is also very easy to chew and swallow. You will be able to time your eating and answering questions with food that is easy to eat.

You should also try to time asking your date any questions. Try to do it when your date has just finished swallowing the food. You should not put your date into an embarrassing moment during the whole dinner and throughout the evening. Should you stumble onto something too personal for your date to answer, you must try to alleviate the situation and quickly change the subject. Try to do this very subtly.

You should not be quiet and just eat your food. Enjoy each other's company and talk about anything. There is no set rule or criteria on what you two should discuss. Let the moments carry you both through the evening. Try very hard not to interrupt each other too much during a conversation. You two could lose your rhythm in discussing various topics. Sometimes this could make some people a little perturbed. There will be plenty of opportunities for both of you to say what you want.

You and your date must turn off your cell phones. It is very rude to have to answer a phone call during your date. You can also shut the ringer on your cell phone. This is a little better if you really need to have the phone ready. If someone should call you, answer the call very brief. Say hello and tell the person you are busy right now and that you will call back tomorrow. You must devote the evening to yourself and your date. There should be nothing else on your mind other than to have a nice time and to learn about each other.

Both of you should never over indulge with drinks. It will slur your speech and you two may say many unintelligent things. Being too drunk is not a very nice thing to see on anybody. Your eyes will start to get red and as well as your facial skin color. It may also make you do things that you two will regret later. The consequences can vary depending on how much you two have drunk.

Never drive a car when you have drunk too much alcohol. You can get into a car accident and get a DUI. Take a taxi to take you and your date home. It is much better to stay alive than to get into a serious car accident while driving home from a date. There will be no more dates for both of you when you do get into an accident.

It is appropriate for both of you to call each other a few days later after the date. There is no steadfast rule on when you should call back. The main thing you two should remember is not to play any mind games with each other. You two do not need to play hard to get with each other. If there is chemistry between you two, then it is important that you both express your true feelings. There may not be any second chances for you two to develop a good relationship.

It would be a good idea for you as man to send your date some flowers. Try to do this on meaningful occasions such as Valentine's Day or her birthday. This is a very good opportunity for you to find out if she really likes by the way she will respond to the flowers. If she mentions that you should not have done it, then you may want to take it very slow with her or even just start looking for someone else. If she is extremely happy about the flowers, she will thank you many times over. Then you know your date does want to see you again.

16

Driving

Beginning Driver

If you are just a beginning driver, you must obey all the rules of the road. Study it very well and practice safe driving all the time. It will take a long time to become very proficient in driving. You will need to log in a lot of driving times. If you do not use the car often, then you must practice when you get home. You can practice for a few minutes going through your neighborhood. If you need someone to go with you, ask a family member to help you.

By practicing, you can become more experienced about the road and the various conditions it can take. You will need years of practice on the various types of people driving on the road. You must pay attention as to how some people react on the road and how they handle potentially dangerous situations. Many drivers will swerve into you if you are in the way. Others may do the right thing and just slow down in their lane and possibly even stop.

Have a calm demeanor whenever you are driving to work and to your home. It is all right to be late, because you are assuring your safety and well-being. In addition, you do not want to be the cause of an accident. You must never hit another driver and especially pedestrians. Always be aware of the passengers inside other cars. You will typically see mothers driving their babies and kids in and SUV or a van. Give them extra room and consideration.

Be a courteous driver and yield to others whenever you can. Let people go through when they are merging with you on the highway. Allow drivers to cut across an intersection when your lane is not moving forward. Do not block off intersections when cars are present. Let them into your lanes or let them pass. Your will be rewarded for your good deeds on the road. You will still get to your destination on time and alive.

The main things to remember are to drive defensively, avoid being hit by people, and always be seen by everybody. Turn your headlights on during cloudy days. You want all the other drivers to see you so that they do not hit you. Make sure all your lights are working properly. Avoid being near reckless drivers and always let them go ahead. Always say to yourself that you do not want to hit anybody, whether somebody else is the cause for it. You want to stay alive for your family and for yourself.

Defensive Driving

You must always drive defensively even if the road conditions are clear and the weather is sunny. Driving is a privilege that you must respect and take very seriously. You are responsible for the lives of the passengers that ride with you. They are entrusting you to take them to the destination alive and well. They are not expecting to become victims of a heinous car accident. They do not want to become statistics that will be reported on the evening news on television.

Many dangerous drivers out on the road do not care about themselves and anyone else. These bad drivers drive as if they own the road and will always risk your life in order to get ahead of everybody. They are always rushing to get to their destination even if there is nothing waiting for them there.

These drivers will weave in and out of the traffic in the city and worst of all on the highway. You have seen these people before in front of you. Watch and observe how they handle their cars and how close they come to other people. They are so reckless they will even cut in front of large, fully loaded trucks.

You can only pray that the bad driver does not hit the truck. You must avoid being close to these drivers, especially when you might be near a truck. This driver may cause the truck to swerve who in turn can hit you. Alternatively, if the bad driver does hit the truck, he may bounce onto your lane and subsequently hit you.

You must never cut in front of a truck whether it is moving slow or fast. Always give way to these large moving vehicles. The reason is that there is so much weight behind the speed that you will be crushed if you are hit. Trucks also cannot stop immediately. They take a long time to slow down because of their sheer size. They will need a lot of road space to come to a complete halt.

A large truck will always crush a car no matter what. These bad drivers just do not seem to understand this simple concept. They think for some reason that they will not be harmed. This is all right as long as they do not drag you into their accidents.

Remember that these events are happening at high speeds. You may not have enough distance to slow down and avoid a bad accident forming in front of you. No amount of air bags can save you totally from a collision with a car or a truck.

Just think of the consequences when you do get into a car accident. You will be extremely lucky if you can walk away from such an accident. You may think that the worst-case scenario is if you are killed in the accident. This is not the case. You could live but in a paralyzed situation or even a coma. Your whole life would have just turned for the worst. You could be bed ridden for the rest of your life or end in a wheelchair with amputated legs. You may not even be able to talk after such an ordeal.

Just think of your loved ones who rely on you. These could be your spouse and children at home. Would you really be willing to get into an accident where you become incapacitated? Now your spouse and children will have to carry the burden of taking care of you.

This is why you must avoid situations where you could have these impending health problems because of a reckless driver. Once you see them, either maintain your speed or slow down a little. Let them go by you and ahead of you. Once they are in front, allow more distance to grow between you and the reckless driver in front. The reason is once an accident happens in front, you will have plenty of time to slow down and possibly stop. Do not let the bad driver claim your life.

Always keep your eyes trained in front of the car. Do not look away even to admire the scenery. Never ever, become a gaper of an accident. That is, do not look at an accident on the highway no matter if it is in your lane or on the other side. If the road is clear in front of you, continue on your way. A car could also hit you if you slow down to view the accident.

Highway Driving

Keep checking your mirrors for the people around you. You need to know where the other drivers are located and what they are doing. Sometimes you will see a speeding car just behind you. This is one of those reckless drivers. If you cannot switch lanes to get out of the way, just maintain your speed or even slow down a bit. This bad driver will flash his headlights or even press the car horn. You should let this impatient driver through while you fall back.

Do not challenge any reckless drivers on the streets. They will just endanger your life by trying to run you off the road. Do not be the one to have road rage because of the increasing numbers of reckless drivers. Remember that wherever you are going, the place will still be there even if you are late. Even if you are late for one hour or ten hours, the place is still there. So relax and do not become angry because you think you are going to be late for work or an appointment. Losing your life is not worth being early.

When a bad driver is exhibiting road rage towards you, just slow down and let him get in front. Make sure you are way behind this driver, possibly two to five miles. However, if this reckless driver is racing you or trying to hurt you with the car, you must get off the highway. You can then get back onto the highway at the next entrance. You have taken away the reason for the reckless driver's road rage to develop against you. That bad driver will go on and find some other person to harass.

You can also change your course for a while until the bad driver has disappeared up ahead. You can go onto a slow lane, which is the far right lane. This is a safer way to go sometimes. Even if there are multiple merge lanes ahead, at least you are not in danger of a fast moving reckless driver.

In fact, you should drive on either the very far right lane or the very far left lane. You must always take one of these lanes and never the middle lane. The cars in the middle lane have a higher probability of being hit from the left and right side. With either far lane, you only have to worry about one lane full of cars. Cars from one lane only will pose the high threat. You have full attention on the road and can better monitor that side. You can better focus your eyes and mind on the cars in one lane.

When you are approaching a curve on the highway or using the exit ramp, you must slow down. Do not maintain your speed or wait for the last second to slow down. You will be endangering yourself and your passengers. Remember in your physics classes that your inertia and momentum is directed forward. You must slow down to ride the curvature of the exit ramp properly. If you get onto the ramp at high speed, the consequence is that you could fly off the ramp and fall into the ditch. In addition, if you start turning the steering wheel wildly about, you could tip over especially if you have an SUV.

The SUV has a higher center of gravity, which makes it more susceptible to roll over due to bad driving. The SUV are good cars to own though, because of the fact that it is higher off the ground. Should a car hit your side or the passenger side, your body is above the bumper of a regular car. Another nice thing about an SUV is that you can see farther ahead of the road. This helps you see the road condition ahead. These are especially good in the snow because of their four-wheel drive options.

City Driving

When you are driving in the city streets, the same rules apply. Always drive defensively. Moreover, you must always make sure you are seen by the cars in front and behind you. Never assume that the cars crossing in front of you have seen you. Even if most of these drivers see you, there are still the bad drivers that will shoot out in front of you. Always have your lights turned on when nightfall is coming. You can also flash your lights to signal that you are moving and that they have a chance to stop. These people are so dangerous that they think you will have enough time to react and stop in order to avoid hitting them.

You must always look at the cars trying to cross at an intersection. Look at the wheels to make sure that it does stop turning. If you can see that it is still moving, then you must slow down your speed because those drivers may just shoot out. There are people out there who will disregard the stop sign and even the traffic light and just continue through.

If you are stopped at a light and it turns green, do not go ahead right away. Watch and make sure that all the cars crossing your path have truly stopped. Never cross if you are not sure because there are some reckless drivers that will shoot across even if the lights are already red. Let these people through and do not allow them to hit you. Their recklessness will catch up with them in the future.

There is a certain psychology about driving cars. If there is about thirty feet or more between you and cars in front, anybody in cars trying to cut across will take the window of opportunity and do it in front of you. What you must do is take away their reason to cut across. Close up the gap slowly and carefully with the cars in front of you. However, you must still leave enough space for braking suddenly. By closing the gap, anybody trying to cut into the lane will see that there is no space. In addition, the driver will see the group of cars and will not challenge the group. They always look for a gap with lone cars to cut in front.

Maintaining Your Car

You must always maintain your car in good working order to maintain a safe driving condition. You will have to replace your all your tires at the same time when they are worn. This will ensure that you have good traction on the road. You must also maintain your brakes to ensure safe stopping.

Do not buy inferior tires and go cheap on the tires. These tires wear out faster. You can always look for sales on the tires and buy rated ones. The same goes for your brakes. Make sure that you properly maintain the brakes at either the dealer or an independent brake repair shop. Fortunately, you do not have to maintain the brakes yearly. The repairs depend on how much you use the car daily.

Driving in Bad Weather

So far, all the discussion above has been around good driving days. There will be days when it will be raining very hard or snowing. When this happens, you must really be more aware of your driving. The reckless drivers will still exhibit their bad driving habits. They have no care about the weather condition and hazardous roads. These drivers will still go back and forth between lanes. They will want to get to their destination even more on time because of the inclement weather.

More than ever, let these reckless drivers pass you. Do not allow yourself to be near them. When they do cause an accident, you must be far away enough so that you will not be involved. There will be a domino effect of cars hitting one another as they approach the accident scene. The cars behind the reckless driver will not have enough time to react. The road conditions are also vastly different on a dry day.

The rain and snow will definitely make the road very slippery. People seem to forget that when water and snow are present, that the tires will lose a lot of their grip. No matter what kind of car you drive, even expensive cars, all the tires are made from the same material. There is no extra gripping power that an expensive car can boast to have. All the cars will lose control and slide around on the wet road.

Always carry a dirt shovel with you during the winter season and if you are in snow region. You will be able to dig yourself out if you do get stuck in the snow. You should also carry extra blankets in the car to keep you warm if you do become stranded. Make sure you have a cellular phone and that it is fully charged everyday.

During these bad weather conditions, the rule that you always have to be seen is very important. You must always turn your headlights on even if there is plenty of daylight to drive. You want everybody to see you on the road so that you are not easily hit.

Should the weather be so very dangerous or you cannot handle the highway, then you must get off and either take the local roads or stop somewhere for a while. You can go to a mini mall or a coffee shop until the weather clears up. Make sure you call your loved ones if you are going to be late from stopping somewhere.

If there are people on the road that seem to need assistance, do not stop. Keep driving because sometimes these could be dangerous traps set up by rapists or abductors. If you really want to help, you can keep driving a bit forward and call the state police. Let the state police investigate and help the people.

17

Convergence

Background on Convergence

Convergence is a phenomenon that happens occasionally to everyone. A convergence happens when two or more people are grouping together towards one place during one range of time. Some of these can have a neutral effect on you while others can be somewhat the start of great pain and suffering. These are events that you must avoid or at least be prepared to handle and manage.

You must train yourself on how to recognize a convergence while it is developing. In time with practice, you will be able to determine events as they are happening that will lead to convergences. By knowing this phenomenon, you will be able to avoid potential accidents that will involve you. You could inconceivably save yourself from a lot of grief and possibly even your life.

The majority of convergences are very frustrating and others can be potentially fatal. The frustrating ones are easier to handle even if you are not trying to determine a convergence. These types can be in a workplace environment or your own family gatherings. You will go through these types during the course of your life.

The more dangerous type of convergence can be happening in a fast pace. The faster the pace, the more chaotic the events are forming around it. Unfortunately, other people create these chaotic events. These are everyday plain people who have discarded respect for themselves. They have become uncaring and self-centered. They have made themselves the central point of everybody else. They will take everything they can and will not care about the consequences.

Highway Convergence

One such type of convergence can lead to accidents where people eventually are harmed. One typical convergence is the traffic that is forming in front of you on a stretch of highway. There are groups of cars and more are even arriving. You can see this from a few miles back. You must slow down since you can hardly avoid it. By doing this, you avoid getting into an accident which could be fatal. This form of convergence is a simplified type, which everyone has experienced on many occasions.

What happens in the highway convergence is that almost all the people are in a hurry to get to their destination. Some people will even try to project their desire to go faster to the person in front. These uncaring people will flash the lights, press the horn and get really close to your bumper. They will even break the law by riding the shoulder and cut in front of you to get a few feet farther ahead. They do this by forcing their way back into the highway lanes. They absolutely do not care what person is inside the car they are cutting in front even if their malevolent behavior causes an accident. This person could have cut off a mother driving with her child. The reckless driver could have injured the mother and her baby with the illegal car lane change.

You can observe this type of event forming in front and see some of the participating people that will cause this event to become into a dangerous situation. You see a disparity of actions happening. Even though the traffic has slowed down, the bad drivers going in and out of the lanes are moving very fast. They persist to gain that extra foot by getting into any open space behind any car that is still creeping along. They are trying to position themselves so that they will be the next in line to move forward. These people are in their own world whenever they are absorbed in a highway convergence.

As you approach the highway convergence, you must begin to slow down. By approaching cautiously, you can see which cars contain the uncaring and reckless drivers. You must identify these drivers and get away from them. You must stay behind these drivers about two to three car lengths.

You must manage the situation when you come across these reckless drivers and let them get ahead while you slow down. The reason is that they will eventually hit someone and cause a major highway accident. Many people are disoriented when caught in a convergence. They will become scared, angry and even vengeful at these bad drivers.

What happens during a convergence is that all the people get distracted very easily. They start looking around too much and start to make irrational decisions. Although, they start asserting their rights of using the highway, their actions are very chaotic. They all think that they all deserve to be there on the highway and that everyone else must give way. They will not yield to anyone or be courteous to other people. These people are very disrespectful and reckless. You must be careful when you see them driving very close to you. You must keep your distance from them when you are caught in this convergence.

The highway convergence is one example, which can become extreme. It is an everyday event during the morning and evening rush hours in major cities. Numerous people keep doing this without regard for the law. The sad thing is that in their collective thinking, they are correct and justified in their actions. The fact of the matter is that they are all negligent people and should not have the privilege of driving a car. They are a dangerous group of people.

As other drivers envelop you in the highway convergence, keep focused on the situation. Keep your mind sharp and stay calm. Drive slowly and let the true natures of the drivers come out in front. Do not provoke any driver. Do not mimic their style of driving by going in and out of the traffic haphazardly.

Remember your training of driving defensively in high school. Always let a car length of space for about every ten miles per hour of speed you that you drive. For example, if you are traveling at around forty miles per hour, you should have about four car lengths in front of you. This length gives you enough time to see any convergences that may form and to deal with it properly.

Office Convergence

Another type of convergence is one that forms when you see a group of office workers gathering. They may be talking by the copying machine or the coffee machine. This convergence is not as dramatic as the highway traffic. In this one, approach the people with caution. It is all right to say hello and get near, but do not stay too long. The people tend to spend a long time talking about nothing in particular. Someone will start a comment, which leads to bad jokes. As the new arrival, you might be the brunt of the comment.

Sometimes, a single person who has bad intentions may sway the office people converging. The crowd around him may start to agree to whatever the person is saying. For example, the conversation could lead to unfounded comments, which then become rumors. You must not become involved with this type of convergence. Go around them and avoid it at all times.

You must approach a group of people cautiously as you come closer to them. What you must do first is to just stand back and observe what is happening. Try to be close but within earshot only. See if you can determine whether they are arguing or not. You must do this exercise to ensure your safety as you become involved in a convergence.

Social Event Convergence

Any social gathering is a convergence, which contain micro-convergences. You could be a nightclub where people gather to dance and enjoy themselves. This convergence should be somewhat organized and contained. However, this is not the case. You will notice that bad things can happen and that you could be caught in the bad situation. Arguments between men and women can flare up. There could be jealous men of other men looking at their girlfriends. Other women may resent women who can dance better than they can. All this can be the cause of a destructive convergence where you can get hurt.

Convergence Frequency

Convergences usually happen more as a periodic occurrence. The extreme worst case is the highway traffic rush hour in the morning and afternoon. You know that this happens from Monday to Friday. Here the ultimate result is loss of human life and destruction of property. Chaos is always present as the people converge on each other.

The office work type is not as dangerous and fatal but often happens. These could happen during morning and afternoon. There will be cases where you will be in a conference room. This is a mandatory convergence and cannot be avoided. Here you must prepare yourself to present facts and to answer any questions. The only thing you can do is to be a professional when attending these convergences. You must make sure you have data to back up your facts. However, it could still be very discomforting to the people converging. There are too many people at one point in time.

You must learn to see the beginning of these convergences. Take notice of the chain of events that have led to a situation that you deem a convergence. Keep a mental note of what types of people are involved and what they were doing. Remember whether they were angry, happy or frustrated. By noting the emotional content of the events, you will be able to realize that a convergence is about to form in front of you or around you. You will be able to keep your distance and stay safe from any harm.

Sometimes you come unto a convergence where you may not be able to lessen the effect. There will not be enough time to go around it. What you must do is to take into heart that you can read and determine that it is forming in front. You must expect the worst and assume that it will happen. When you do realize this type of convergence in front, you can then try to avoid it. You can stop in your tracks and look for another path that you can take. You must do this while you still have some control over some events.

There is no need to panic. By staying back and keeping your distance, you can be relatively safe. You must stay calm at all times. With a clear mind, you will have the advantage over everyone that is rushing around in a chaotic manner. You will be more astute and have better judgment in making decisions. You will make mature decisions that will even save your life.

Epilogue

In closing, I hope that this condensed guidebook has provided some insights for Asians living in America. I hope that many Asians can become better acclimated to living in America, whether they have been living in America for years or are new immigrants.

For all the Asians who have read this book, I hope I have given you enough insightful advice on how to have a stable family unit and how to have a successful life in America. My family and I have had to overcome many obstacles especially at work. I know that new Asians moving to America will have the same problems I have encountered.

I know that this book will tremendously help in your children's education and tuition costs. It will help you at work and ultimately in pursuing a patent. I have given short and straightforward advices so that you will not be too overwhelmed. I know that many people do not want to read too many pages in order to get a simple advice.

Leonardo D. Moral

6056 N. Whipple

Chicago, IL 60659

0-595-32044-9

www.ingramcontent.com/pod-product-compliance
Lightning Source LLC
Chambersburg PA
CBHW020243290526
45784CB00003B/1094